TIGERS

.... AND PICTURES OF MANY MORE

PAUL JEFFORD

Steyning, July 2004.

Photograph Mark Jefford

First published 2015 by
Paul and Joyce Jefford
Whitegates Farm
Hatton
Market Rasen
Lincolnshire
LN8 5LS
telephone 01673 858536
email pauljoyce.jefford@btinternet.com

By the same author *There's Something about a Maxi*
ISBN 978–0–9567622–0–7

ISBN 978–0–9567622–1–4

Typeset by Joyce Jefford

Printed and bound by
Arbons House
47 Water Street
Suffolk
CO10 9RN

CONTENTS

FOREWORD

I hope this memento of Southdown's Eastern Coach Works-bodied Leyland PS1/1s will be seen as a worthy contribution to the wider celebration of the Southdown Centenary. It was first conceived as a tribute to GUF 727 on reaching her 60th birthday in 2007 – a project put aside first when I ran out of time and then while I was working on *There's Something About a Maxi*.

Apart from my wife's contributions that add some variety of style and emphasis, the text is my own, though I have naturally consulted published material as well as indulging in some very enjoyable delving in the archives.

All the typesetting preparation has been undertaken by my long-suffering wife, who has ably coped with the haphazard nature of my drafting.

The photographs are a mix of those taken by others many years ago, and a considerable number of previously unpublished images including quite a few from my personal collection.

An omission enforced by the apparent absence of records is information about maintenance, mechanical overhaul, engine changes and the like. Nor have details of costs and prices been easy to come by. I wonder whether present-day enthusiasts will be able to preserve such information for my own generation's posterity.

Paul Jefford
29 April 2015

CHAPTER ONE – WHY?

I am hoping there will be something in this book to interest everyone. If those who are knowledgeable about buses like it, I shall be happy. If it appeals to people from my native Sussex I shall be very well content. And if it attracts the many people for whom a bus journey has never been a part of everyday life I shall be especially pleased.

I am sometimes asked why I am so interested in old vehicles. Why do I want to preserve them? Why buses? And why in particular the two buses we own? Briefly, it is because we think it worthwhile to preserve and promote our country's transport heritage. It is because these were Southdown vehicles. It is because they are Leylands. And it is because not many Leylands had Eastern Coach Works bodies. Chapter Eighteen explains it all in detail.

Soon after moving north from my native Sussex many years ago I was in a company of people in rural Lancashire. Before long somebody asked "Where do you coom from?" "Sussex." "Aw, Soosecks, thought that were a hen." "OK, where are you from?" "Lehland." "Oh, I thought that was a bus." This little exchange explains a lot. Just as the other chap had been aware of the *Light Sussex* breed of domestic fowl, so I had known *Leyland* as a make of buses and lorries long before I learned it was the name of a town in Lancashire! I had grown up in the territory of Southdown Motor Services Ltd, for whom any make of bus other than Leyland was the exception.

Bus books come in all manner of styles. My preference is for something which adds to my knowledge in a bright and entertaining way. And which reminds me that without people buses are nothing more than inanimate machines. So they need setting in context to bring out their personality and charm – two commodities rarely absent from the

Southdown fleet during my formative years.

This book is written with that in mind. It gives a few insights into the problems and pleasures of preserving and exhibiting historic vehicles. It recounts the story of 677 right through from delivery in 1947 to the present day. It offers an account of the rest of 677's batch, GUF 727–HCD 451, along with a photo gallery providing 78 images of them all in various guises and roles. It also includes some details about our other bus, Royal Tiger MUF 650, which we have repatriated from Malta after 40 years of service there.

And why is the book entitled *Our Southdown Tigers*? Well, 677 has never been just mine! At first I bought her jointly with another would-be preservationist and since then have shared her with my wife and partner in all things Joyce, who refuses to become a bus widow. Being of the "if-you-can't-beat-'em-join-'em" persuasion she has loyally participated in all things 677 over the years – even to the extent of obtaining a PSV driver's licence after I got mine in the mid -1980s.

Would I dare say "My"*?*

Photograph John Child

CHAPTER TWO – IN SERVICE WITH SOUTHDOWN

This book is not the place to go in depth into the history of Southdown, Leyland or Eastern Coach Works. Suffice it to say that the year which has seen 677 reach her 68th birthday has also witnessed the passing of 100 years since the setting up of Southdown, 200 years since the beginnings of Leyland and 95 years since the start of the Coach Works.

Southdown had bought Leyland vehicles in a big way since the 1920s, and its love affair with the PS1 was no great cause for surprise. Bodywork was another matter. Coaching services had been suspended during World War II, and 125 coaches had been requisitioned.

This is the earliest photograph I have of 677 – dark but full of atmosphere. On receiving it in 2003 I was able to track down the photographer, who told me it was taken at Victoria Coach Station some time early in 1948. Note sliding top windows and painted radiator.

Supplied by D A Jones

[Note: I prefer to include images of less than ideal quality where their omission would leave a gap in the story.]

Express services were resumed in March 1946, and replacements were needed for the vehicles that had been requisitioned. So to meet urgent needs several different body builders were used for the 125 PS1s taken into stock. Eastern Coach Works supplied the earliest batch of coaches to arrive. Our Tiger was numerically the first of these.

At home in Worthing garage.

Copyright Southdown Enthusiasts' Club

On the London Service.

Copyright Robert F Mack

On Worthing seafront for an evening trip.

Photographer and Copyright holder unknown

In Horsham garage, 13 October 1956. By 22 February 1955 GUF 727's destination screens, windows and seats had been changed to convert her to single deck bus configuration, and her fleet number changed from 1227 to 677. In April 1955 she was allocated to Horsham, where she remained until retiring from the Southdown fleet on 17 October 1960.

Photograph Michael H C Baker

Off to Maplehurst.

Photograph W J Haynes, Copyright Southdown Enthusiasts' Club

677 retained her higher ratio back axle after leaving Worthing for bus work, so was still perfectly capable of holding her own on the express services.

Is she going to London again?

Copyright Alan Lambert collection

Here, with its interpretation, is a somewhat time-worn relic of her Horsham years found in a crevice when cleaning up inside the saloon. It is a Setright ticket of a type used by Southdown for many years. The machine is one of the first post-war batch of Setrights that Southdown bought in 1948 and may well have survived to be decimalised in 1971. Previously Southdown had TIM Major machines.

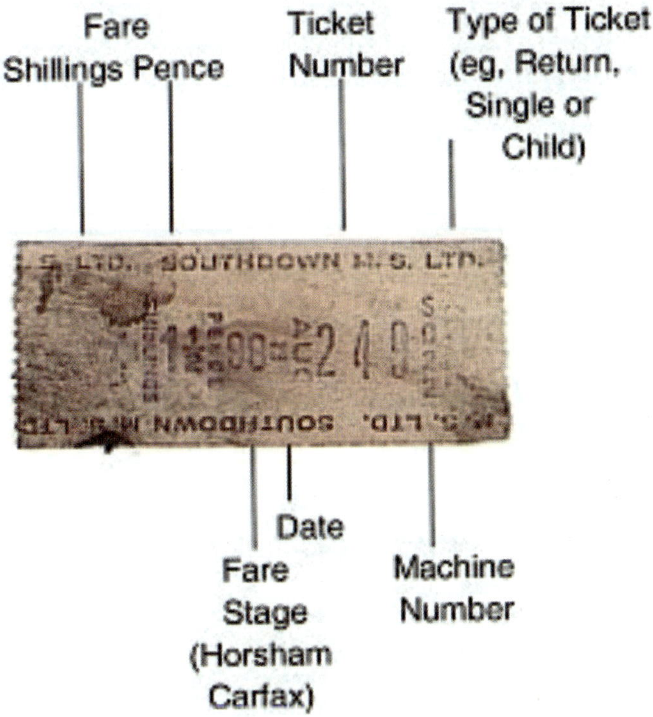

Incidentally, Setright is not a concocted brand name as one might think. It is the name of the proprietor of the firm that made the machines. LJK Setright, the well known motoring writer, was his son.

Sure she is now a bus, but this looks suspiciously like her old stamping ground.

Photograph Kevin Lane, Copyright Southdown Enthusiasts' Club

Don't know where, don't know when.

Copyright Roy Marshall Collection

Note the flashers on the vehicle behind 677, which indicate that she was either 687, GUF 731, or 689, HCD 449. 677's were fitted in 1976, as I do not consider driving without them is a viable option in today's traffic conditions; they match 689's.

Copyright Southdown Enthusiasts' Club

Conductor giving guidance.

Photograph Surfleet Transport Photographs

Specially drawn by Don Vincent

CHAPTER THREE – DONKEY CLUB INTERLUDE

Following full-time service with Southdown, 677 passed to the Donkey Club, a local charity involved in providing holidays for people with disabilities. At that time she acquired a new set of tyres which served for the next 40 years. On joining the Donkey Club she was sprayed all over in dull grey with blue lettering.

For about three years she led a semi-active life taking people out for weekly rides. Many of her seats were removed to make way for wheel chairs. Then the Donkey Club lost its driver, and 677 was left sitting unused and in decline in a farm shed until found in 1972 by a local enthusiast. He advertised his wish to share her with anyone willing to put up part of the purchase price. Why did that catch my eye?

Because by then I had been under the influence of omnibuphilia for well over 20 years.

This Donkey is a Tiger, y'know!

Copyright probably Southdown Enthusiasts' Club

Look closely on the left for the passengers in wheel chairs, who boarded the bus via a ramp through the emergency door.

Photographer and Copyright holder unknown

CHAPTER FOUR – TIGER AWAKENED

That local enthusiast was David Coxwell. I soon contacted him. He took me to see the bus he had found. There she sat in the shed, a drab, grey bus surrounded by a sea of brown. Beech leaves? No, onion skins. I never discovered – indeed I never got round to asking – the reason for this strange combination of bus and bulbs.

Surrounded by onion skins.

Photograph Paul Jefford

Anyway, there she was, a Tiger bearing the title *Donkey Club Express*, with a great cut-out of a donkey's head occupying the position below the radiator filler cap that should have proudly proclaimed the name of either her birth place in Lancashire or her first owner's name in Sussex. She was covered in dust, bore signs of battle with objects harder than herself, showed the effects of long exposure to rain coming through broken windows of her residence, but was otherwise complete. The batteries were still there, though long since dead and past resuscitation. Several tyres were completely flat. We were told she had not been out for some eight years.

Was this a bus I wanted a share in? I was not too sure. She wasn't a 1400. My ideal was Southdown's Harrington-bodied pre-war Leyland Tiger single deckers, 1400–1485. My first memories of these was on Service 80 as they were running in the mid 1940s. Grey roofs, rear quarter lights, wartime temporary standee seating – "Pass right down the car please. Room for 80 standing." (All of their buses and coaches were "cars" in Southdown-speak).

1426, DCD 326, showing rear quarter lights. Note the tin hats and blanked out destination screen.

Photograph Alan Lambert

The 1400s had been worked hard during World War II and were subsequently rebuilt by a range of bodybuilders. They rated as dual purpose saloons with comfortable seats and well appointed interiors. From them, I suppose, stems my preference for single deckers. A single decker wending its way along country lanes has a cosier, friendlier atmosphere than an impersonal urban double decker that has "them" upstairs and "us" inside.

But by 1973 the 1400s had ail long since gone. Not one preserved – if only I had bought a couple as they came out of service in the 1950s instead of saving up for a new car! How short-sighted we sometimes are. That new Ford Popular lasted only eleven years and a mere 61,000 miles, though it did still have three of its original tyres. And the PS1s had always sounded nice. Maybe I did want a share in this one. I went home to "think about it".

I had recollections of 677 in her first years on the road, a long time before I became consciously interested in buses. Later came a period in the 1950s when she had carried a tired and hungry Paul Jefford on the last stage of his long journey home from London at the end of a lengthy working day. That was enough. Yes, I did want a share in this bus.

The asking price was just the scrap value of £50. This included the removed seats that had been kept in store. I shelled out £25 and became the owner of half of 677. After a while, my co-owner got married and decided he no longer needed half of 677. So I paid over another £25 to become – the sole owner? Well not quite, I remain half-owner to this day. My good wife Joyce has always gone halves with me in everything we do.

I have never believed in keeping vehicles in the open, and I had nowhere to keep a bus under cover at home. So she stayed where she was for a modest rent until the owner of the farm decided to put it on the market. I drained the diesel tank and put in fresh fuel. I arranged temporary accommodation on a farm at Slinfold. The farmer and I connected up a couple of his combine harvester batteries, switched on, pressed the starter, and the old girl fired on the instant – then spluttered to a stop. Oh dear. Wasn't she going to go? However with a bit of twiddling with the injectors we got the engine running. The next stage was to get the shed doors open to drive her out. But not before a mass of undergrowth and a small tree had been removed.

677 about to leave her home of many years.

Photograph Paul Jefford

To drive the bus home we needed insurance: I duly took out a policy under the Historic Commercial Vehicle Society (HCVS) scheme. A vehicle on the road also needs to be taxed. To tax a vehicle one needs an MOT certificate. To obtain an MOT certificate we need to drive to a testing station. A chicken and egg situation. A new situation for Joyce and me. Bus preservation can involve some steep learning curves. I made enquiries and learned that if we pre-booked an MOT we were allowed, for obvious reasons, to drive to the testing station without a tax disc. So we booked an MOT in our home town. The original logbook had been lost, so a duplicate was obtained. We were ready to remove 677 from her home of some fifteen years.

It was a damp, grey November day, but 677 has a diesel engine, so we didn't have to worry about damp leads. The combine batteries were connected up. She started in a great cloud of white smoke. We pumped up the tyres and drove carefully away. Those tyres had been down long enough to have flat places still on them even when inflated, so along the road we went, bump, bump, bump until the flat places rounded out. A faulty diaphragm in the governor left the engine racing away when the accelerator was released, making gear changing with no synchromesh something of a problem. But in due course we got safely parked up in our drive at home, ready to complete the journey to the testing station next morning.

There the governor diaphragm was replaced. A pair of reflectors was fitted at the rear to meet the current legal requirements. A new light bulb – and we had an MOT certificate. Just like that.

"There's your bed of nails" said Mr Spooner of Jackson Bros in Horsham as I collected her from that MOT. Bed of nails she might have seemed to some. To me 677 was an old friend that had sometimes carried me home from work 20 years before, and I wanted to preserve her.

A lot of hard work, a lot of money spent in the ensuing 40 years. Sure. But bed of nails? Not at all. A better analogy would be a magic carpet. A nice sunny day, with a decent stretch of road, traffic flowing reasonably and driver in good form – enjoyment, euphony, euphoria would not be words too strong to describe the experience. Ask any of at least a score of eager volunteers who have spent time at the wheel of our pet Tiger. They will all tell you the same. And when you sit in the bus behind them you can see their grins stretching not just to their eyes, not just to their ears, but in very truth right round the back of their heads. If you don't believe me, come aboard one day and see for yourself!

Soon to be on the road again, 1 June 1976.
Photograph Diana Gilmartin

Bodywork needing some attention, 1 June 1976.
Photograph Diana Gilmartin

For the next few months 677 was stored outside under a tarpaulin. Before taking her out again I had the sump off for cleaning. I recollect a scene on our back lawn in which Joyce rose bodily in the air while supposedly holding down the sump as I removed the drain plug with a big spanner and a four-foot length of iron pipe. I also recall ending any thoughts a white nylon shirt might have had of remaining white when I inadvertently rolled on my back in a pool of used engine oil.

Interior facing rear, as found except for the two passengers, 1 June 1976.

Photograph Diana Gilmartin

Very soon she moved on to a new home in Eastbourne. In due course flashing indicators were fitted as a necessary modification to ensure safety in the more demanding traffic conditions of the period. By the summer of 1976 our bus was back on the road.

Receiving attention in Wales, 31 August 1976.

Photograph Joyce Jefford

She accompanied us on a family holiday in mid-Wales and spent three weeks parked in a farmyard, where I removed the *Donkey Club Express* lettering, made up temporary blinds saying *Private* from spare pieces of wallpaper scrounged from my parents (which served for over 20 years), made up the battery cages to fit a set of ex-RT batteries I had obtained at Cobham, got some wiring repairs done and a few other jobs.

Back in Sussex 677 returned to Eastbourne, also attending an Open Day at Southdown's Portslade central works, and going to the very first rally at Hellingly before heading into hibernation.

Portslade Open Day, 4 September 1976.

Photograph Joyce Jefford

Bus and boys at the first Hellingly rally, 28 September 1976.

Photograph Joyce Jefford

CHAPTER FIVE – THE WAITING YEARS

I guess for many people the biggest headache in preserving a large vehicle is finding storage space in the right place. Keeping 677 was no exception. We had been able to find nothing nearer to home than Eastbourne, 40 miles away, which meant that we could not work on the bus in odd moments. Joyce and I had jobs and small children, so there were not so many occasions when we could take a full day out. We settled into a routine of getting batteries charged and starting up 677 about twice a year – which she was always willing enough to do. Then in 1980 we moved even further away, to Sheffield.

In 1982 I had a request to borrow 677 from Dennis Odd, who kept an ex-Jersey Morris Commercial in the same building. He duly paid for tax (normal car rate for historic vehicles in those days) and MOT. One place he took 677 was the Amberley Museum.

At Amberley in 1982. Note the flashing indicators below the rear lights.

Photograph supplied by Dennis Odd

At that time some one had the kindness to relieve 677 of her ECW body number plate and the *8 standing pas-*

sengers notice over the passenger door. If anyone reading this is in a position to return them I should be very glad to have them back, please, with no questions asked.

Having moved north I needed storage much nearer than Eastbourne, and eventually I found a place for 677 in a new transport museum in Buxton.

Leaving Wenham's.

Photograph Joyce Jefford

The pattern of occasional visits to start her up continued, and we did get some other work done. Inspection revealed serious deterioration of the interior panelling below the windows, which was made of plywood covered in rep. The panels we took out made a cheerful bonfire in the museum back yard. I didn't like destroying items that had been part of the bus for so many years, but they really were irredeemable.

All too soon the museum proprietor decided he wanted 677's space for some other exhibit. And not too long after that the museum closed down. 677 went into storage at nearby Harpur Hill. Before very long her space was required for a cold store, and the search for accommodation was on again.

At Harpur Hill.

Photograph Mark Jefford

The next move was to a furniture store in Stockport, on the transport museum proprietor's trade plates. He insisted on driving her himself. And just as well he did, for he was stopped by a policeman somewhere around Hazel Grove. By the time I pulled in behind in the car the arm of the law was clearly satisfied and cheerfully assented when I said "Do you like her?" Actually she was no pretty sight at all, but her natural charm was clearly showing through the dust of several years in store!

Again the occasional visit regime continued, and again the old girl never failed to start on the button. In all those years in storage she received no mechanical attention other than occasional maintenance.

Meanwhile there were stirrings on the preservation scene in Sheffield. I began to make contacts, gave the occasional helping hand and in 1985 found a place for 677 in the South Yorkshire Transport Collection at Chapletown.

En route to Sheffield – storming up the hill at Surprise View.
Photograph Joyce Jefford

No longer was a major expedition required for going to work on her. One of the first things I did was to fit locks on cab and saloon doors. She began to go out and about, attending an Open Day at the South Yorkshire Transport Greenland Road garage on 10 August 1985.

Packing up after the Greenland Road garage Open Day.
Photograph Joyce Jefford

There followed a rub down, some touching in and a quick coat of green paint.

She got her picture in the *Sheffield Star*.

Getting ready for repainting, 26 August 1985. Mark on roof; Joyce at side; Paul, Ken and John left to right at front.
Photograph Sheffield Newspapers Ltd Copyright Johnston Press

She won a prize at an Open Day and went on park and ride duties.

On duty with the Monocoach, 28 September 1985.
Photograph Joyce Jefford

It was all too good to last. Within a year the South Yorkshire Transport Collection broke up and the premises were vacated. Despite promises of accommodation elsewhere, I received four weeks notice to quit. Something had to be done. Something was done, quickly. Within two weeks 677 was on her way to mid-Wales again.

Passing through Newport, Shropshire, 19 July 1986.
Photograph Mark Jefford

She spent the next year comfortably settled in a farmer's sheep shed.

Day trip out while in Wales, 30 August 1986.

Photograph Joyce Jefford

Leaving Wales in 1987.

Photograph Joyce Jefford

Back in Sheffield efforts were being made to found a bus museum, which culminated in the setting up of the Sheffield Bus Museum Trust using a section of the former Tinsley Tram Shed, the home of the first Sheffield tram cars in 1874. On Saturday 13 June 1987, 677 stopped masquerading as a sheep in rural Wales and pretended instead to be a tramcar in England's fourth largest city. She was now garaged a mere eight miles from home.

Arriving at Sheffield Bus Museum, former Tinsley Tram Shed.

Photograph Joyce Jefford

CHAPTER SIX – RESTORATION AFOOT

Eight miles from home. Now we can get down to some serious restoration. Now we can get the dent out of that front wing, remove and replace those dented panels, renew rotten timber, tidy up the seats, sort out the rear corner panels, straighten out the bumper .... Well, of course it didn't quite work out like that. Joyce and I were taking bus driving lessons, getting our PSV licences, working on house and garden, taking holidays, keeping our cars up to scratch, making regular visits to Aberdeen – 776 miles in a weekend. There were many other things to do. 677 did not often get first priority.

Mark Jofford hammering out dents in the rear wings.
Photograph Joyce Jefford

We did make a start. The front wing got straightened up, and the rear corners. In 1990 we determined to take the old girl to the Southdown 75th Anniversary celebrations at Amberley. We removed damaged side panels, we repaired pillars, we bought new panels, had them cut and shaped.

As the day approached it began to become more and more obvious that we were not going to have everything ready in time. There were mishaps. A window fell out of its frame and broke, so we lost time getting new glass. Joyce went sick. Eventually we gave up, and Mark and I set off to Amberley by car.

Off with the dented panels and radiator, August 1990.

Photographs Mark Jefford

Failing to meet our deadline after such a flurry of activity was bound to create an anticlimax. Little more was done for several years.

As can be seen in earlier pictures, 677's radiator shell had taken a bash – from running into a gate apparently – while in the hands of the Donkey Club. It also needed re-chroming. So the shell would have to come off. Undo a few nuts or screws? Oh no. To separate the shell from the grill and radiator, it was necessary to remove the whole assembly including radiator bodily from the chassis. No mean feat. It needed four people to draw it off. The first move after separating the shell from the rest of the assembly was to strip off the old chrome.

An establishment in the Barnsley area was located, shell duly taken to be stripped, then collected and taken to a firm in Sheffield for straightening, minor repair and polishing. So far, so good. Back to Barnsley for re-chroming. No problem? On the contrary, big problem. The chap who had stripped it then declared he'd got so much sludge in the bottom of his dipping tank that there wasn't enough room to immerse the shell. And he'd not be cleaning out the tank in the foreseeable future. Shiny brass shell returned to Tinsley in all its glory.

Rather than leave a gaping hole we decided to place the shell in position without the radiator, and 677 took on a distinctly fire engine-like appearance. This is how she explained it:

A Radical Apology

Please do not think I'm such an ass
Because I have a nose of brass.
The truth is that the plater's well
Won't take my radiator shell.
So chance and time in dour alliance
Have made me like a fire appliance.
Please Note: before again I roam
I shall be off in search of chrome.

Wearing her brass radiator, May 1991.

Photograph Mark Jefford

That's the way things stayed while the search was on for someone who could undertake a re-chroming job. Enquiries in Manchester drew a blank, but eventually a man in Wolverhampton said he could take on the job, which in due course was done and the refurbished shell was carefully conveyed to Tinsley to be kept under wraps inside the bus awaiting the day of re-fitting – a day several years off.

In 1994 we moved to Lincolnshire, again leaving 677 too far from home to work on. She stayed on in Tinsley. We weren't even getting to start her up. We had taken on a larger home, with twelve acres of land. So many other things to do! Would that bus ever get restored? Not until we were finally able to keep her at home.

In due course we had space to store the bus under cover at our own house. Now for the first time in all those years she would be at hand to work on at any convenient moment. But we couldn't take her on the road with umpteen panels off, no radiator on, batteries down.

We considered sorting all this out at Tinsley, but decided it would be easier – as well as saving rent – to take her to Lincolnshire without further ado.

Being driven out of Tinsley Tram Shed, April 1996 ....

Photograph Joyce Jefford

.... onto the low-loader's platform.

Photograph Joyce Jefford

Home in our shed at last, April 1996.

Photograph Joyce Jefford

Eventually the stimulus came that pushed us into action again. In the Spring of 1997 we received an advance invitation to attend the Leyland Titan Day at Amberley on 21 September that year. At this point I hand over the narrative to my wife.

Joyce painted herself as well as 677!

Photograph Paul Jefford

"There I was, green paint all over my arms and driving our Montego, J727 GUF, and caravan through central London. Why? Well, Alan Lambert had invited 677 to the Titan Day at Amberley. She is a Leyland Tiger PS1 – a single deck version of the Titan. That was enough for her and Paul – 'We're going if we can!' HELP! 677 was minus radiator, several hoses, six side panels, most of the trim and four batteries. She needed servicing, lubrication, an oil change, an MOT and a total repaint. At least she was at home.

"Where to start? A detailed list would have been too discouraging. So it was just main areas needing attention that we listed. Times were estimated for each area, balanced against known commitments for the next few months, and we decided we might just be able to meet the deadline.

"We couldn't start work on 677 immediately because we had some urgent tasks to do around the house and garden. Then other things delayed us further: we decided we'd better seal the shed floor to keep the dust down; another week was lost when the drive had an unplanned resurface; an unexpected funeral cropped up. So the unscheduled delays continued.

"But we had started – we'd got the panels, some wheel arch trim, a couple of fan belts and a drum of oil; put the batteries on to charge; borrowed a grease gun nipple and roped in our brother-in-law to help service and grease her and get the radiator on.

"When the deadline for entry arrived, we took the plunge, telling each other that 677 could go in primer if need be. The MOT looked just about obtainable in the time. More late nights, decisions to leave some items for now, urgent enquiries to the Lincolnshire Vintage Vehicle Society (LVVS) on the lines of 'Where can we get ...?' or 'Who can do a Class V MOT quickly?', and 677 began to look more like a bus again.

Radiator – paint drying in the Dining Room, and now reinstalled.

Photographs Joyce and Mark Jefford

"On went the radiator – it seems to weigh a ton even when empty and some of the hose clips are in impossible places! On went the batteries. The tyres were inflated. On went the panels: the new rechargeable electric drill had a baptism not of fire but overwork. We virtually lived in the shed – surrounded by tools, paint, brushes, rags, mugs .... and the cordless telephone was a permanent fixture.

"Some LVVS members were taking down the Bolton TD1, WH 1553, with Steve Milner's Lincoln PD2, RFE 416, as back-up vehicle, on Friday and invited us to travel in convoy. Sounded a good idea to us – 677 had not been on the road for seven years.

"The MOT was booked for Wednesday 17 September. By then the radiator had been filled, back axle oil topped up and general preparations made; our son Mark had checked lighting/electrics, replaced some fuses, cleaned glass and chrome; and so Paul drove off to Lincoln for MOT. I followed in the car 'just in case'. No problems en route or there – she passed first time at a recorded mileage of 37,414.

New panels on for MOT.

Photograph Mark Jefford

"So back home to start painting. She was already filled (in places) and primed (in other places). Volunteers had been roped in to rub up the exterior beading and clean down the roof, two of whom had helped with the first repaint in 1986.

"There was no time for undercoat. Several hours were spent stirring the top coat we had bought seven years before, and then, from Paul with 24 hours before off 'You'd better start on the cream – I'll start on the roof with the dark green.' ME, paint the bus? I am not a very good painter – don't have a steady enough hand, but no choice, really. So, since the cream edged up to the beading (which was off) I started. 'Light green next, please – I'm still on the roof.' 'OK, but you'll have to do the cutting-in.'

Working on through the night.

Photograph Mark Jefford

"Came zero hour on Friday morning – 04.00 – half of 677 still to paint and the day was wet and foggy. A call to Steve – 'The weather's too wet for our new paint – have a good journey and we'll hope to see you tomorrow.'

"Then we took stock. 'If we have a couple of hours sleep, we might manage to finish the painting ....?' We did. Then hasty packing of car and caravan, an even hastier bath (hence the green paint still on my arm several days later), another few hours sleep and on a bright dry Saturday morning, 677 trundled out of the yard – back to Sussex for the first time in fifteen years."

CHAPTER SEVEN – AMBERLEY – DAY OF THE TITANS

We've done it! We've done it! 677 is back on the road again. Repainted – in Southdown green and cream. This must be for real. We are on the road again, going to Sussex, with me driving 677 and Joyce in charge of the car and caravan.

She continues the story.

"My task was driving the car and towing the caravan. The main problem was keeping down to 677's speed – 35 mph. Because she'd not been on the road for such a time, I followed all the way as insurance. We need not have worried. The only problem was hold-ups from coach drivers and other people coming for a chat whenever we parked up for a break.

See what I mean?

Photograph Joyce Jefford

"Having arrived at Amberley, we set up the caravan, received a visitor, were joined by Mark, who'd spent the afternoon in the Midlands, and so to bed. As much as we had found of the trim went on with the minimum number of screws next morning with Alan hustling us down to her stand."

The Titan Day was staged to celebrate the 70th anniversary of the launch of the Leyland Titan bus in 1927. Designed by GJ Rackham the Titan was a landmark in the development of the double deck bus and set a trend for at least the three decades that followed. Successive models of the Titan were produced in their thousands right up to 1969 and were used throughout the UK and well beyond. As an interesting aside, Mr Rackham left Leyland and soon joined AEC (the Associated Equipment Company) "makers of London's buses" where he designed the AEC Regent, the Titan's main competitor for the next 30 years.

Some of the vehicles at Amberley.

Photograph Joyce Jefford

Only about a dozen examples of the original Titan model TD1 remain in the UK, and seven were brought together at Amberley, one from Glasgow, one from Jersey, one (now resident in Lincoln) from Bolton and four formerly belonging to Southdown. Another was booked to come but failed to turn up. The one from Lincoln went down and back under her own power – petrol at five mpg – with no problems at all.

Also represented at Amberley were most of the succeeding Titan models from the 1930s – TD2, TD3, TD4, TD5 and the post-war models PD1, PD2 and PD3, several of these again coming from the Southdown fleet. Most were on service round the museum site during the afternoon. The pre -war Leyland engine was almost as smooth in diesel as in petrol form, and the melody of the gearbox is well-nigh impossible to describe to the uninitiated. Suffice it to say that to those of us who had known them in their heyday the sound of all those Titans going up and down the gears on the slope at Amberley were the sweetest of music, evoking memories of many a journey in the days of our youth. The gargling of the PDs of course provided an equal uplift for those who were young in the 1960s and 70s.

There were also Tigers of several generations producing the same harmonies, a few Lions, too, close relations of the Tigers, and at 16.00 there was a grand parade – no small feat for some 35 vehicles in such a small area, and one not done before at Amberley. But we just drove off, as buses do, one behind the other, pulled up at the other end, as buses do, each with his nose two inches from the other fellow's tail, proceeded sedately on our way and returned to our places, no trouble at all – and what a field day for the photographers, the camcorders and the audio enthusiasts.

At the Titan Day at Amberley.

Photograph Mark Jefford

It was not a big event, there were no prizes, but the Titan Day embodied all that is best in rallying: a beautiful, sunny September day; a picturesque setting; a representative range of vehicles, well presented and carefully driven; good but not excessive organisation; a clear and comprehensible theme; a happy and welcoming atmosphere; plenty of rides for the visitors, with something on the move almost all the time. The look of pure joy on the faces of some folk at seeing 677 on home ground again was reward enough. All the work of the preceding months had been worthwhile. For me, Amberley Titan Day was the event of the year.

Joyce continues the story.

"Monday morning saw us off up north in convoy: Bolton TD1, Birmingham PD2, 677, our car and caravan and the Lincoln PD2 to bring up the rear. The Birmingham bus left the procession near Dorking, but the rest of us continued right through central London. I lost the others just after Oxford Street, but kept going northwards and eventually spotted the roof of the Lincoln PD2 far ahead. They waited for me as soon as they could park, and we had no further problems.

"Came South Mimms and a refreshment stop. Some swapping of drivers and passengers took place. Paul elected to ride in 677 and, later on, in the TD1, handing over the driving of 677 to Steve Milner, who subsequently reported 'I don't know who or what was purring the loudest, me or the PS1.' At Grantham Services, we got ourselves sorted out, and there we parted company with the LVVS buses."

Thank you, Joyce. I couldn't have told the tale better myself.

CHAPTER EIGHT – PUSSY CAT, PUSSY CAT, WHERE HAVE YOU BEEN?

For us the highlight of 1998 was undoubtedly taking our pet Tiger to Buckingham Palace. Clearly 677 has something that I haven't got. For 35 years I served Queen and country and never got so much as an invitation to a Royal Garden Party. That PS1 has only to appear at Amberley with a shiny radiator, a few new panels and a new coat of paint, and she attracts enough attention to produce an invitation to the inner quadrangle of the Royal residence. There must be a moral in it somewhere. I guess in all walks of life a few moments of showing off will often win a great deal more recognition than years and years of unremitting slog. But I digress.

Again I will let Joyce take up the narrative.

"1998 was supposed to be the year 677 did NOT get much time and/or money. My grey Ferguson was my priority, although I think Paul cherished ideas of one of the FB Victors receiving the benefit of our limited resources. But 'the best laid schemes of mice and men gang aft a-gley.'

"In April we received a telephone call. 'I saw your bus at Amberley in September. Would you be interested in taking it to Buckingham Palace?' 'Yes.' Then queries. 'Why?' 'When?' 'Doing what?' 'Taking passengers from Buckingham Palace to Waterloo on Tuesday 2 June. More details to follow.' After a few more phone calls the facts began to emerge. A Save The Children Fund fund-raising event was planned, to consist of a reception at Buckingham Palace hosted by the Princess Royal, followed by dinner on the Orient Express at Waterloo Station. The idea was to transfer the participants from one venue to the other by 'vintage' bus, the first thought having been to use former Southdown vehicles, including the Amberley fleet.

"As far as we were concerned, 677 had been made

presentable for Amberley externally, but the interior was another matter. Also, it was more than time for her to proclaim again that she was once a Southdown vehicle. So another planning session, and this year a list. Signwriting, batteries, seats and interior panels were the main items. We had run to Amberley with two car batteries and a jump lead in the saloon – so two new heavy duty ones were purchased.

"In the meantime, members of the LVVS had come to our rescue once again. The names of a signwriter and an upholsterer resulted in 677 being signwritten since we could obtain neither the correct transfers nor vinyls, so Paul made templates of the letters, and six seats were resewn.

Still bearing the signwriter's markings.

Photograph Joyce Jefford

"Then all was put on hold – we were rather far away from London, and no one from Stagecoach was available to check the suitability of 677's interior for carrying VIPs in their good clothes! So we relaxed, took a couple of days off to attend the Carrington Rally, and turned our minds to other things. We shouldn't have done. On Friday 29 May we had another telephone call. 'Would you like to come after all, seeing how much preparation you've already done?' What could we say but 'Yes'? Once again action stations and very little sleep. It was preparing for Amberley all over again.

"We knew we had not yet cured 677 of leaks – don't know where the rain comes in, but come in it does – so we weren't inclined to re-cover the side panels permanently, though we have the authentic material to do so; but something had to be done – bare framework was not going to be acceptable. After much thought and hunting round at home, we decided on hessian-covered hardboard panels as a temporary measure, which we duly assembled on the dining room floor and screwed into place in the bus.

"We toured Lincoln trying to match the brown seat frame paint and found something that was 'near enough' for now. No time for rechroming, so the worst of the chrome seat back rails were rubbed down a bit and then touched in with silver paint where needed.

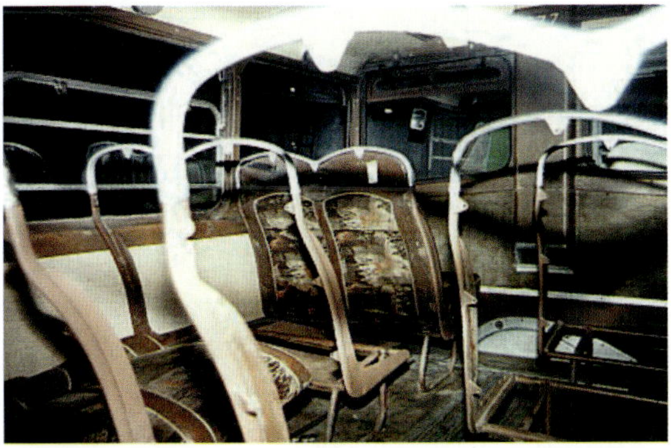

Study in seat frames.

Photograph Mark Jefford

"Our brother-in-law was urgently summoned to assist with servicing once again. Mark fixed the new batteries into two of the underfloor battery cages.

"Then the floor got its first scrub for some 35 years. It looked much better, but the linoleum on the radiused panels was very tatty. No time for replacement, so another search and a strip of old stair carpet and a bottle of Copydex later, 677 had a linoleum floor with a carpet edging.

"Seats and seat backs were reassembled – the frames are slightly sprung, so screw holes didn't want to line up easily, but eventually 677 had a full complement of seats once more, and all firmly bolted down.

"Early Monday morning found me upside down on the steps painting the step well and the inside of the saloon door. So once again I set off south with green paint on me and barely dry paint on 677 – we actually used the emergency door until we reached Grantham.

"Down the A1 we went – me cleaning the inside of the windows on the way. I had a go at driving, but seemed to have lost the knack of changing gear! We spent the night at South Mimms, and so great was the interest in 677 by coach and lorry drivers that it took us a full hour to get away to our room. Mark joined us there later in the evening.

"Rain overnight meant that not much could be done on Tuesday morning, but it stopped about mid-day. Mark polished the chrome radiator, I wiped off the cream paintwork, Paul made a sign for the front saying 'WATERLOO', and the sun came out. By the time we set off for Bressenden Place, even the roads were dry, so we were spick and span for our evening's work.

"We arrived at Bressenden Place several hours too early, but were very pleased to find Bill Thorneycroft there awaiting his bus – the Dennis from Amberley. A friendly traffic warden told us where we could park – in the coach park on Millbank. We checked our route for the evening and parked up. We were soon joined by Leyland Beadle, MUF 488, and Leyland Cub, CUF 404, so pictures were taken of three ex-Southdown vehicles parked in two modern coach spaces."

Again I couldn't have told a better tale myself.

Assembling at Millbank, 2 June 1998.

Photograph Mark Jefford

After parking up for a while, we left Millbank in company with the Beadle and the Cub, travelling together to Bressenden Place. A representative of Stagecoach South greeted us there and gave us stickers to display; one was the Save The Children Fund logo, and the other a girl's name, Lucille – which we eventually recognised as the name of the Orient Express Pullman carriage on which our allotted passengers were assigned to dine. All the vehicles then departed for the Palace.

Through to the inner quadrangle.

Photograph Mark Jefford

The traffic was held to give us a clear run in through the great front gates, across the outer courtyard where the Changing of the Guard takes place, and in through a tiny archway to the inner quadrangle where we lined up. There were eleven vehicles in all, dating from 1927 to mid-1950s. Once inside we circled round and lined up in two rows facing the end we had come in.

Conductress Joyce.

Photograph Paul Jefford

It seems reasonable to assume that we were on ground not normally trodden by the humble motor bus. And one could be forgiven for thinking that those old vehicles were of the same opinion. It was a brilliant scene, with the low evening sun slanting in across the quadrangle and highlighting the patchwork of colours presented by the two line-ups. The greens and yellow of the four Southdown cars, the maroon of the Bedford SB and the Dennis Dart, the red and cream of the Dennis Falcon, the blue and yellow of the Eastbourne AEC Regal, the Tilling green of the Dennis Mace, the dark green of the London Country RF and the superb brown and yellow of the Surrey Motors Regal combined in a gleaming kaleidoscope of glossy paintwork that drew admiring glances from windows all round the quadrangle.

Awaiting our passengers.

Photograph R E Gray

The wait of half an hour or so for the guests to emerge from the Palace gave drivers and crew the opportunity to photograph each others' vehicles – or just to chat. At one stage a large red Bentley, 1 ANN, entered the quadrangle, and the uniformed chauffeur was soon chatting amiably with us mere bus drivers.

One of our drivers admitted to being beyond the age at which the male of the human species can be sure of immunity from urgency problems of a particular kind and became a little concerned during our long wait. Negotiations were in hand for entry to the Palace for a very limited and specific purpose when the guests began to emerge, so all further thought of entry was hastily abandoned. A pity. It was probably the closest that any of us had ever come to getting inside the Royal residence.

We have it on good authority that a few of the guests leaped for joy when they saw the kind of transport lined up for them. They walked across the quadrangle to their waiting vehicles, each group in charge of a hostess. Brian (now Sir Brian) Souter of Stagecoach made a brief inspection. As the buses filled they left the quadrangle through another archway as small as the first, across the outer courtyard towards the crowds outside of the railings. Now we knew how they looked from the inside. Out through the great gates, turn right, massed police holding the traffic for us again, and off to Waterloo.

Leaving the gates of Buckingham Palace, 2 June 1998.
Photograph Mark Jefford

The route was straightforward – round the Queen Victoria Memorial, along the Spur Road, Birdcage Walk, Great George Street, one side of Parliament Square, Bridge Street, over Westminster Bridge, along Westminster Bridge Road, into York Road, Addington Street, back to Westminster Bridge Road and down the tunnel to the station platforms.

Once at the platform entrance we all disembarked our passengers and disappeared in our several directions – in our case to South Mimms, followed by return to Lincolnshire next morning. Everyone agreed it had been a fabulous evening, a unique occasion unlikely to be repeated. An additional satisfaction was that the events of the evening raised £500,000 for the Save The Children Fund. Altogether an experience that made the rest of the year a bit of an anticlimax.

CHAPTER NINE – LINCOLNSHIRE LOCALES

From the time we had her back on the road, our Tiger was in demand by the LVVS for its Open Days at the Lincolnshire Road Transport Museum, held twice a year – at Easter and the beginning of November. On these occasions she usually went to the Museum the day before and returned when the Open Day was over. On the day she would participate in the free bus services put on by the Society, including the park and ride facilities between Museum and local parking places and the railway station, runs into Lincoln city centre and some short country tours.

This usually involved about 100 miles per Open Day – 50 miles on the free bus services and a 40-mile round trip from home to the Museum. Driving on the day was by qualified drivers on the Society's approved list. 677 was always popular with drivers and passengers alike, and almost invariably every seat was full. She has attended to date ten November Open Days and four at Easter, the first in November 1997 and the latest in 2012. Here are two pictures of her at the Museum for her first Open Day.

Rear wheel arches and lettering still to be added ....

Photograph Joyce Jefford

.... also bumper and rear apron.

Photograph Joyce Jefford

By her next attendance in November 1998 bumper brackets had been removed and straightened. A new rear apron panel had also been fabricated, the bumper straightened and refitted, the cab interior repainted and the saloon door closer refitted.

Straightening the bumper brackets.

Photograph Joyce Jefford

The November 1999 Open Day celebrated 70 years of Lincolnshire Road Car. For this occasion we fitted a replica front destination blind based in part on a Horsham garage original.

We were unable to attend the next Open Day, Easter 2000, and when we returned to collect 677 the public were all gone, but so was our bus. Just arriving from "one last trip". Only months later did we discover that "last trip" had been a country tour for the day's volunteers.

Many people have taken Open Day pictures of 677 since then, frequently posting them on the internet. This one was taken at the November 2012 event.

Photograph John Child

Another LVVS activity in which 677 has participated from time to time is the free park and ride facility between the car parks and the main gate at the annual RAF Waddington International Air Show. On these occasions Society and members' vehicles scurry up and down a section of the perimeter road picking up and dropping off passengers all day in exactly the way they would have done in their working lives.

Demand gets very heavy at times, at which periods the crews run a constant shuttle service until the queues are cleared. After two days everyone is worn out, but it is a rewarding thing to be out there running what is a very real full scale service with yesteryear's buses.

Sometimes passengers get so fascinated with our historic vehicles that they are reluctant to leave the bus when they get to their destination. I once had a small boy yelling blue murder "I don't want to get off Bertie the Bus!" Another time a passenger coming on board after observing the place names on my destination screen decided that in his youth he would have been riding this bus over that route and insisted on taking a double journey on 677 before even going into the Air Show.

Passengers alighting for a day at the Air Show.

Photograph John Child

In September 2004 she also attended a rather belated gathering at the Lincolnshire Road Transport Museum to celebrate its achievement of Registered Museum Status. A short trip followed for some of our former colleagues from Sheffield.

In 1998, 1999, 2000, 2002 and 2003 we took 677 to the Lincolnshire Steam and Vintage Rally at the Showground which is one of the bigger steam and tractor events in the country, with plenty of cars and lorries, but very few buses. One other PS1 to appear for a few years was former East Kent coach, CFN 73, with a Park Royal body like those on 25 of Southdown's other PS1s.

An added attraction on the first night is an organ concert for exhibitors only, when engines and organs pair up and play on into the night. The music somehow sounds better in the night air. The darkness shows up to best advantage all the coloured light bulbs and shiny, barley-sugar-twist brasswork on the showmen's engines. But when people and engines are both perambulating, the sudden realisation of a multi-ton piece of obsolete machinery silently sidling up out of the night behind one, ready to pass within an inch of one's ear, is an experience more easily felt than tell't!

In 1999 we were invited to join an impromptu run by the lorry fraternity into Lincoln city after the Rally gates had closed, to line up along the quayside at Brayford Pool.

The next year the highlight of the show for us was an informal Saturday evening run between the last arena event and the start of the organ concert. We pulled into a car park at Sturton-by-Stow and parked up between a couple of Sentinel diesel lorries from the Rally. A Sentinel steamer was also there, but nothing to prepare us for what was to follow.

Parked with the Sentinels, 1999.

Photograph Joyce Jefford

One after another, in ones and twos, no fewer than fourteen more vehicles piled into that yard and parked up:

eleven Sentinel steamers in all colours, shapes and sizes, two Foden steam wagons and one large Foden road locomotive! We had happened on the annual gathering of the Sentinel Owners' Club, apparently held at a different show each year. The scene also attracted a good turnout of the local population. At one point during the general proceedings, two of the steamers were observed quietly regaling themselves from the public hydrant in the middle of the road.

For an hour or more we savoured the sounds and smells of steam from the roads of yesteryear, were reminded again of once familiar hauliers' names and liveries and wondered once more at the dedication of the men and women who so evidently had put hours and hours and hours of labour into restoring, maintaining and running these impressive machines. Whenever I see Sentinel steamers in their ultimate state of design and development, silent, smooth and speedy – or indeed some of those fast, light steam cars that go skipping about on rally fields – I never fail to reflect what a pity it seems that the steam option was allowed to die so completely in favour of the internal combustion engine.

Not many buses at the Lincolnshire Steam and Vintage Rally, 21 August 2004.

Photograph Joyce Jefford

Another local event we attended several times with some of our vehicles was the Sleaford Historic Car and Motorcycle Show in early September. 677 went in 2003 and 2004. I particularly recall 2004 when we also took our historic Maxi.

At Sleaford Historic Car and Motorcycle Show, 2004.
Photograph Joyce Jefford

From the Lincolnshire Road Transport Museum also came the Austin 18 and the Morris Minor Co-op van, while a Ford Zephyr 4, and a Ford Capri were contributed by members. This meant we had enough vehicles to have a Club Stand. During the day we made a couple of short trips off site with 677. There was a good variety of cars, commercials and motorcycles, with several unusual vehicles. Radio controlled models whizzed around at terrifying speed, occasionally hopping froglike over anything that dared stand in their way.

As usual, many folk came on board 677, looking, smelling, touching and generally savouring the 1940s-1950s ambience of our pet Tiger. We never quite cease to marvel at the way many people identify with our vehicles. The one essential for enjoyment seems to be that they have met one, or something similar, at some past period of their lives. What often draws people to 677 in particular is that the interior is still largely original. The sun shone, the vehicles gleamed, the punters swarmed around, we enjoyed visits from local LVVS members.

We have sometimes staged a very small event at home, where members and vehicles of the Austin Maxi Owners Club and the LVVS – and any other interesting vehicles (and people) we can rope in – gather to talk and eat and maybe go for a ride, etc.

Lion and Tiger cheek by jowl. Difficult to realise that the Lion is only 20 years older than 677. Pictured at 3 July 2004 Maxi Meet.

Photograph Joyce Jefford

Over the years our Tiger was out and about on various occasions for specific purposes.

One day in September 1999, Joyce and I, dressed up in our Southdown uniforms, took 677 to Lincoln for a photocall. The Editor of one of the national bus enthusiasts' magazines was doing a feature on the LVVS collection, and we were invited to join in. We were duly photographed with 677 in a leafy lane and appeared in the next edition. Now bus magazine editors take pictures of buses, and sometimes bus owners take pictures of bus magazine editors taking pictures .... get it? We duly sent to said Editor a picture of himself standing on a chair photographing a line up of buses in the Lincolnshire Road Transport Museum. We have not yet seen it in his magazine, but (with his permission) it certainly went into the LVVS magazine *Con-Rod*.

Our sales stand, Tallington, 20 May 2000.
Photograph Joyce Jefford

Sometimes a local Rally is a good chance to make a meaningful test run. So it was in 2000, when an invitation to the Tallington Steam and Country Festival, near Peterborough (but still in Lincolnshire) on 20 May also provided an increasingly rare opportunity to have our sales stand out. 677 behaved impeccably, so we thought we were all set fine for the big trip to Portsmouth.

On another occasion we carried an equally satisfied group of passengers to a school prom, where the competition consisted of other historic vehicles, stretched limos and I know not what.

Another outing for 677 came in May 2006, when she provided a round-the-site passenger service at the Lincolnshire Showground on an Open Day put on by local haulier and driving school, Denby Transport. On the due date, Joyce and I set off with 677 for the Showground, via our local paper shop. Little the Jefford household does seems to raise eyebrows in the neighbourhood. 677's looming presence outside the village store evinced no more than an unsurprised "Is that your bus outside?"

Denby's Open Day, Lincolnshire Showground, 20 May 2006.
Photograph Joyce Jefford

Before going on bus duty Joyce and I each had our lorry drive in a big Scania artic – something Joyce had wanted to do for years. She found it very like a car to drive, except for the size, and even that wasn't much longer or wider than the car and caravan outfit she was thoroughly used to driving.

Our Tiger once also aspired to the role of TV celebrity. In 2006 she was invited to participate in the BBC2 Castle in the Country programme, appearing during the afternoon of 3 November. Yet another thing that bus has got us into.

22 April 2007 was the date of the Federation of British Historic Vehicle Clubs' annual Drive It Day, when owners of historic vehicles are encouraged to take their prized machines out on the road for all to see.

It was also 677's 60th birthday. Way back in austerity-ridden 1947 she had been one of the 2,646 new buses and coaches delivered in the UK. She had lived three times as long as most of her contemporaries, so there was cause for celebration.

Here are a couple of views of her pausing on her birthday outing along the edge of the Lincolnshire Wolds. It is difficult in 2015 to realize that in 1947 new cars were unobtainable for most people and public transport reigned supreme. Nor can we now conceive how it was then profitable to run a 31-seater coach with a crew of two.

677 is 60, 22 April 2007 – FBHVC Drive It Day.
Photograph Mark Jefford

Proudly proclaiming her longevity, 22 April 2007.
Photograph Mark Jefford

An outing on 21 May 2011 was to a late celebration of Mark's birthday with a visit to a local collection at Rand. Here 677 met up again with the OB that had belonged to an LVVS member and had graced the Museum when we first came to Lincolnshire. A lot of catching-up and swapping of stories ensued with other people we knew.

677 catching up with an old friend.

Photograph Joyce Jefford

CHAPTER TEN – FARTHER AFIELD

The Autumn of 1999 found us busy preparing 677 for the Ian Allan 50, Manchester 20 Event at the Museum of Transport Greater Manchester. We offered 677 for this event three weeks beforehand, and began to sort out a few jobs that needed doing – bell not working, attention to reflectors, checking oil levels, tyres, batteries, refuelling, fixing battery access flaps, measuring beading for bumper at rear, polishing radiator grille, getting the bus to the Lincolnshire Road Transport Museum for Open Day and home again.

All this in between a hectic programme of woodshed renovation and a visit to a Ruston car tucked away in Lincoln, to say nothing of getting another driver on 677's insurance to get her from Lincoln to Manchester because we were to be in Sussex the day before the event and moving on to Scotland immediately after. Phew? Well not really – just a normal couple of weeks in the lives of an active retired couple. If it hadn't been all this, something else would have kept us equally busy!

Just to ensure we kept up the pace, no sooner had we arrived at Manchester than I was asked if we would like 677 to have a run in service, so 12.00 saw us setting off with a load to Heaton Park, where we paused for a photocall before returning to the Museum. She was well received, and we even had three chaps on board saying "We were riding in this bus at Lincoln last week!"

In September 2002 it was time to take 677 to the Sheffield Transport Rally at Meadowhall. 677 had not returned to Tinsley since getting back on the road again in 1997. She was particularly keen to meet her old next-door neighbour there, a Yorkshire Woollen District Brush-bodied Leyland PS1, HD 7905, which had recently emerged from a long programme of restoration.

Tinsley neighbours reunited.

Photograph Joyce Jefford

She did one round trip between the rally site and the Bus Museum, with a very full load each way, at the end of which one officer of the Sheffield Bus Museum Trust emerged with a faraway look in his eyes chanting "Three first gear starts, three first gear starts, three first gear starts." Hypnotised – that bus's powers to bewitch have to be observed to be believed! It was good to meet old acquaintances again, and we enjoyed our day.

Five half-cab single deckers, Meadowhall, September 2002.

Photograph Joyce Jefford

After preparation that included a new exhaust section and curing a rear axle oil leak, 17 August 2007 saw us set out on the 305-mile run from Hatton to Lathalmond. We had three drivers for 677, so did the journey in one day, arriving at the Scottish Vintage Bus Museum just over eleven hours after leaving home, with no problems on the way.

We had gone to fly the flag for the LVVS, to say "Thank you" to the people from Lathalmond who regularly bring a bus down to the November LVVS Open Days. With a nominal top speed of 43 mph our bus was faster than any of the other vehicles in the Museum at that time.

677 parked up at the Scottish Vintage Bus Museum, August 2007.

Photograph Joyce Jefford

As usual, 677 attracted a lot of interest. She went on several trips to Dunfermline over the weekend, well loaded for each journey. She also suffered the indignity "after hours" of Joyce and Mark having a go at driving her – with mixed success.

Bright and early on the Monday morning we all set out for another uneventful, albeit long, journey home. A fuel consumption calculation at this point showed that the old girl had averaged 12.01 miles per gallon over the last 1,427 miles of mixed long distance and local running. On a long run she has been known to achieve 18 mpg.

Both the LVVS and myself have been members of the HCVS for many years. So Joyce and I decided to take 677 to the HCVS Golden Jubilee Rally at the National Motor Museum in 2008. The HCVS is one year older than the LVVS, and we flew the LVVS flag as well as our own, succeeding so well in this that we were caught by Michael Banfield in the middle of the rally field wearing LVVS and Southdown badges with nary an HCVS badge in sight!

After our usual preparations (which included a special trip to Lincoln to obtain a new 25 litre drum of SAE 30 for an engine oil change only to discover on getting back home we'd had one in the boot all the time) we set off at a most uncomfortably early hour on 25 July. Joyce drove the Montego with caravan leaving me alone in 677, as no one from the LVVS had taken up our offer of seats.

Two ECW bodies on show at Beaulieu, July 2008.
Photograph Joyce Jefford

About 125 vehicles showed up over the two days. There was an interesting range of commercials dating from between 1908 and 1986, emergency and military vehicles from 1907 to 1985 and buses and coaches from 1922 to 1980. Entries came from as near as the National Motor Museum on the other side of the hedge and as far away as

Yorkshire, Tyne and Wear and Lincolnshire.

We thought the event deserved a larger number of entries. It was relaxing and informal with plenty of opportunity for networking, catching up with people we hadn't seen for years and browsing in the autojumble and sales stands. One entry was GS 76, MXX 376, whose owners were offering rides into the New Forest, which we enjoyed.

We also had free tickets to the National Motor Museum, Palace House and Beaulieu Abbey, including the lovely mediaeval *Domus* in which on 14 July 1957 was held a meeting, chaired by Sir Henry Spurrier, that led to the setting up of the Historic Commercial Vehicle Club in 1958.

The journey down had seen horrendous hold ups on the M25, M3 and M27, but the only hold up on the way home was being flagged down by a coach driver in a lay-by wanting to know if I had any spare PS1 lights. You never know what's coming next when out with historic vehicles. As I came into one service area on the way home a couple of coach drivers rushed across saying fluid was dripping from underneath. Leaking hose? Couldn't see anything. Top of radiator cool as a cucumber. Lifted the cap. Not even steaming after a steady 72 minutes driving.

Passengers boarding 677 for a local journey at Wythall, 28 August 2012.

Photograph Joyce Jefford

Supporting the National Association of Road Transport Museums in celebrating its 30th birthday on 28 August 2012, we took 677 to the event at The Transport Museum Wythall. She went on a couple of local tours completely full, as usual, and she enjoyed the day as much as we did!

CHAPTER ELEVEN – OH GEAR!

One of 677's longer trips was to Hampshire and Sussex in 2000. She had been invited to a special Southdown Day at the City of Portsmouth Preserved Transport Depot, Portsmouth Harbour.

After oil changes, greasing, battery checks etc and the usual scramble to get away, Joyce and I set off in 677 for Warwick, where we had booked in car, caravan and bus on a small caravan site near the M40. As we left home the rain began. As we went on the rain increased. As we went further the rain increased even more. The windscreen wiper was going full pelt, large bubbles were blowing under the windscreen, water was coming into the cab, water was coming into the saloon. Driver's knees were getting wet, passenger's feet got damp.

It wasn't that we didn't realise that 677 was not entirely waterproof, but we did wish that the weather wouldn't throw a typical English summer's day on the very date we were obliged to be on the open road for hours. However, every cloud has a silver lining: most people boarding 677 for the first time swoon away at her period aroma – leather, moquette and all those lovely 1940s things – and we had long suspected that quite a bit of it has to do with the slow drying time of that bit of real carpet on the floor!

Our overnight parking place.

Photograph Joyce Jefford

On reaching our destination, we found a good concrete hard standing for 677, but the middle of the caravan field had become an unscheduled ornamental lake, so when Mark arrived a little later with the Montego and caravan we took a firm decision to eschew the soggy field and set up the 'van in the farm yard. In all this time the windows of heaven remained open and the waters prevailed. We went to sleep to the sound of pelting raindrops on the caravan roof. Through all this our faithful Tiger had behaved totally dependably, and we slept soundly.

In the morning the sun shone brightly. We rose, packed up, checked our respective steeds and cheerfully departed in good time to make our rendezvous at the M40 Warwick Services with AUF 670, former Southdown Leyland Titan TD3 970, which was coming from the West Midlands. At the first junction I went to change down in our trusty Tiger when – what on earth, I suddenly had an orbiting gear lever. Yes, it was going round and round! I drifted to a halt by the roadside. Mark hopped out, peered underneath. I wiggled the gear lever about, and we found it had become disconnected and trying to rotate at every movement. Those familiar with the Leyland PS1 will know that the gear lever has a bend in it – had it been straight, then we might not have had so much of a problem. I managed to push it down a bit to reconnect, and we carried on to our rendezvous.

We pulled out the spanners and had another look under 677's cab floor, but there was nothing obvious we could do on the spot. A passing driver of a modern coach dropped by wanting to borrow a screwdriver to adjust his windscreen wiper – "I know you chaps with old vehicles always carry plenty of tools" (insult to 677 really, whose behaviour that day was very uncharacteristic). He did nothing to help us, of course, and it so happened that we didn't have the right screwdriver for him either.

The appointed meeting hour came and went without any sign of 970. We eventually contacted Southsea by mobile. Manifest distress that end. A pregnant silence so profound that I could hear the kittens being born one by one. Nothing had been heard about 970. Two other vehicles had already dropped out. Now 677. Who next? The half cabs would be swamped by those modern Queen Marys and Bristol VRs after all!

An hour after the planned meeting time I spied in the distance the familiar shape of a 1940s East Lancs front dome, and minutes later 970 bundled in. She had had a late start because of battery problems.

A quick refuel.

Photograph Joyce Jefford

Then two green and yellow buses pulled out of a green and yellow BP filling station and made a breathless dash for Portsmouth, followed by a white Montego Estate towing a 1973 Sprite Musketeer caravan. I gave 970 the lead as the slower vehicle. She went like a rocket on easy ground, but died much more quickly than 677 on the hills, so I had to make extra gear changes with that dodgy gear lever, but we managed well enough.

This was the view from behind.

Photograph Joyce Jefford

I paid a further price for ceding the lead by being led to Portsmouth rather than Farlington. Though our directions were perfectly clear, 970's party had obviously been before and headed straight for Broad Street. I was sure we were on the wrong road but I just had to follow. Other fellow eventually pulled up. Fortunately we had been spotted off course and were soon being led back to the Stagecoach garage at Farlington.

Parked in Farlington garage.

Photograph Joyce Jefford

We duly arrived, parked up 677 in the distinguished company of the two veteran open-top double deckers owned by Stagecoach – Southdown 0135, CD 7045, 1922 Leyland G7 with 1928 Short Bros body; and 0813, UF 4813, 1929 Leyland TD1/Brush – and went off to find our caravan site. The next morning 677 got a pressure wash and we set off for Portsmouth Harbour. Guess what, that gear lever started playing up again, and I completed most of the run in third – tuneful, yes, but slow.

We reached the Depot in Broad Street. Quite hard to believe we were actually there, the event had seemed so dogged by failures to materialise; just to add to it, 0813 had also refused to start that morning and missed the show due to a punctured fuel pipe and a Leyland Leopard/Harrington coach was reported stuck in the mud in East Sussex. Other exhibits arrived, including 517 (the Dennis 30 hundredweight) and 928 (Leyland TD1/Short) from Amberley. I reported my gear lever trouble. Various people offered help, which soon materialised in the shape of Bruce Macphee. He got into his ever-present boiler suit, went underneath, and put things together again. We had a very pleasant day, meeting people and vehicles, some for the first time, and 677 gave a brief ride round the locality during the afternoon.

At Old Portsmouth, 28 May 2000.

Photograph Bruce Oliver

At close of play we returned to Farlington, left 677 there while we collected our caravan and duly set off with bus, car and 'van along the A27 for Laughton, where 677 was booked to attend the Cuckoo Spring Fayre next day. All went well, we paused for a break near Arundel, on again, no problems, until – wait for it – as we approached the Sompting bypass, that gear lever went loose again – on a roundabout. Luckily there was a layby long enough to take bus, car and caravan, and 677 coasted into it. Mark went underneath but could achieve nothing more than getting his hands greasy. What should we do? I stirred the pudding in the cab, got a gear and set off, Mark leaping aboard just in time.

I managed to get up through the gears into top again – and that's where I intended to stay. In top gear. No more chances to be taken. My gear lever was loose. Stay in the same gear at any price. We still had many miles to go, and before long it would be dark. It wouldn't stress the old girl too much to take the roundabouts in top. And we might be lucky with the traffic lights. We had dual carriageway and shouldn't be holding up the traffic. So it was just the hills we had to worry about. Now anyone familiar with the A27 between Worthing and Lewes knows that it goes up and down quite a few times, up and down some quite steep hills, up and down some quite long hills – hills quite long enough and steep enough to demand third gear in a PS1, loaded or not. But if we failed to make a gear change we were certain to come to a halt. So? We could only have a go.

And go we did, as never had I seen a PS1 driven before. Steady enough on the level, to be sure, no reason otherwise. But when we see Old Erringham ahead, Mile Oak, Hangleton, Falmer, hit the floorboards on the downhill run – up to 40, 50, maybe a little more (top speed of 43 is theoretical). Down the hills she bounced, never mind the noise, never mind the bumps, never mind the rattles. Get her going, keep her moving. Foot to the floorboards, keep that accelerator foot hard, hard down. Keep her going. Give her all the fuel you can, she would need it. We bottomed out and began to climb, willingly at first, gradually slower as we climbed, past the point where no amount of coaxing, no amount of willpower, nothing more the driver could do, would urge that engine on. We got slower. W-e g-o-t s-l-o-w-e-r, w--e g--o--t s--l--o--w--e--r, well below the point where we should have changed down. Still she chugged on, protesting a bit, deader and deader but still slogging on, as only a diesel engine could. Still she kept going, never stalling, no suggestion of clutch slip, just doggedly on, and on, and .... she was picking up speed again. We had made it. Forward! Next hill, and the whole nail biting, but ultimately exhilarating experience was repeated.

And so we went. All along the back of Shoreham, Brighton, down into Lewes, round the roundabouts, up Malling Hill, all the way to the Ringmer road junction. In top gear every inch of the way. What a journey! What a bus! We thought 677 was priceless before. That performance made her doubly priceless. And what eventually halted her? Not the hills, surely? No, just the need to stop for oncoming traffic before we could make a right turn. I managed to get bottom, and the run up from the junction to the top of the hill was made in that gear, never mind how much following traffic. Then I managed to get up through to top again, and we duly arrived at Laughton well after dark.

We picked our way through the mud to the entrance, Mark dragged someone out of the beer tent to tell us where to park. "Just go to the end of the road and stay there. We'll sort you out in the morning." So we parked up one behind the other just as we had come in and set up the caravan for the night. When we woke in the morning we saw where we were – right at the end of the new road that the steamroller fraternity had been busy making up during the show. Elsewhere the field was inches deep in the kind of high quality, creamy milk-chocolate mousse mud that only good Sussex clay could produce. We set up bus, caravan and car all together on a clean patch of grass – between the lawn mower racing and the tractor pull. I came back to 677 after a look around the show to find half a busload of folk in conversation.

Parked at the end of the new road.

Photograph Joyce Jefford

Bruce Macphee and Susan had turned up in response to an SOS from us that morning, as had a former neighbour of ours in Horsham, who in turn lit upon a couple of his old neighbours from Hailsham right there in our bus. Bruce got going on that gear lever again. We ended the day by taking 677 to Bruce's shed not far away and leaving her there for him to take a longer look at the gear lever.

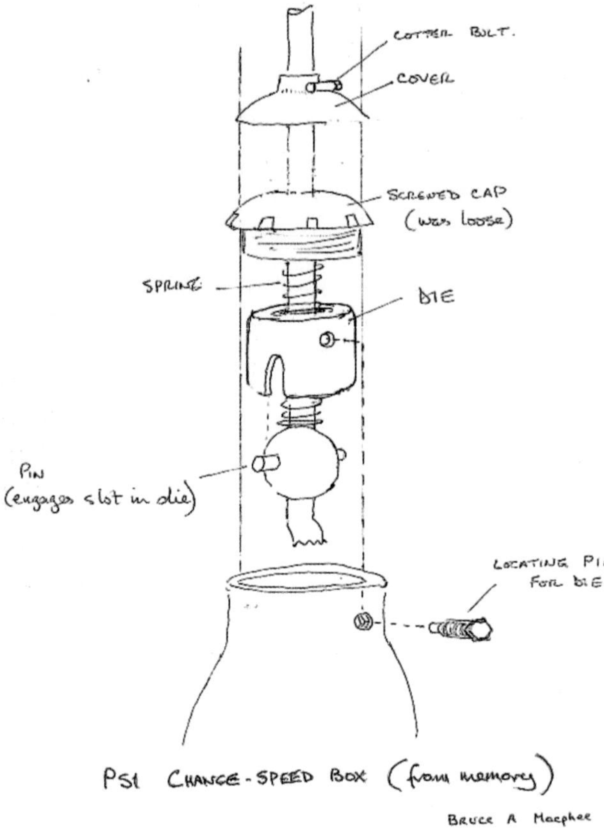

Drawing kindly supplied by Bruce Macphee

Later we returned to Sussex where we took the opportunity to repaint 677's centre band in a deeper shade of cream. We collected 677, gear lever now repaired. Bruce had also adjusted the clutch stop and wanted a test run, so we took her for a little run through some of East Sussex's loveliest villages on a beautiful sunny summer afternoon (yes there were just a few in the Millennium year). All went well with, I do declare, 677 wearing a grin every bit as broad as that of the men. Joyce was looking happy too, but she doesn't admit quite so readily to being swept off her feet by mere buses.

The scene was now set for 677's return home – but not by any direct route, oh no. Chris Pearce had been trying for a while to persuade us to bring 677 to the Worthing Rally – and there she was already in Sussex. It was not to be, for we had booked her into The Leyland Society's Second Annual Gathering to be held at the Wroughton 2000 Nostalgia Show on the same day. But we could route our journey from East Sussex to Swindon via Worthing, so on the afternoon of 27 July 677 duly turned up on Worthing sea front, right by her old home for a photocall with a handful of ex-Southdown PD3s. Plenty of space for 677, but Joyce was going demented demanding what she was supposed to do with the Montego and caravan for an hour or so! A simple enough solution was found for this little problem: the Montego and caravan were neatly parked up in 677's old home, while 677 enjoyed the limelight out in the street.

After waiting in vain for the promised attendance of local media representatives, the familiar convoy of bus, Montego and caravan got under way again for Swindon, Joyce being less than pleased when I headed away from Worthing Dome down the bus lane! Bus, car and caravan were duly reunited near the Offington roundabout. With no further problems apart from an unintended detour approaching Wroughton, we duly reached our destination in the dark with the site gates firmly closed and locked. So we parked up bus and car, set up caravan and settled down for the night by the roadside. We were not alone.

The next morning gates were opened and we trailed across the airfield to join the line at the check-in point, only to be told we couldn't book in 677 until 14.30. But they did let us take the caravan through to the campsite, so we set up the 'van and went exploring. Many people will know that Wroughton is a disused airfield used by the Science Museum to store a substantial part of its transport collection, from VC10 aircraft down to horse drawn fire engines, including some interesting buses.

When we were eventually allowed through, we were made very welcome on the Leyland Society stand. The next day the show opened, and we met up with some old acquaintances, and made some new ones, both people and vehicles. One star was Mike Sutcliffe's recently restored Leyland charabanc. Another was Fraser Clayton's Leyland Cheetah, featured in most of the bus magazines about that time.

There were two fire engines from the Bristol brigade that had not been seen together for years. There was a trio of bonneted Leyland Comet lorries, including one we knew from the Sheffield Bus Museum. It was good, too, to see 873, UF 6473, the Southdown TD1 driven up from Amberley, and the Leyland Cub, CUF 404. That evening a very pleasant barbecue was put on for Leyland Society members. There also was the usual opportunity to ride in each other's vehicles round the airfield. On the second morning of the show in came LAE 13, Leyland PD1/ECW, a double deck counterpart of 677, so we arranged a hasty reshuffle to get the two of them parked up side by side for the day.

677 with LAE 13.

Photograph Joyce Jefford

The last morning we took advantage of the wide open spaces of the airfield to give Joyce a refresher course in driving 677. The last time she had tried on the road she just could not change gear, so was now much heartened to find that with a little advice and encouragement from a loyal husband, she could do it again – and again, and again. So the next time you see 677 bombing along the A27 it could have Joyce at the wheel.

CHAPTER TWELVE – BACK TO ROOTS

Out of the blue early in May 2002 came a phone call from Chris Pearce saying he had just received permission for a display of former Southdown vehicles in the Stagecoach garage in Worthing in connection with the Queen's Golden Jubilee running day, on 1 June. Several preserved ex-Southdown vehicles would be operating a bus service for real between Worthing and Brighton. He really would like to have our bus there.

Now 677 had been having a real good rest during the foot-and-mouth disease year and was still sitting quietly with all her rear wheels off following fitting of new tyres. On SORN, out of MOT, and the last time the headlights were switched on, smoke had appeared. Although she had been started up regularly she had not been on the road since September 2000.

We were going to have to work fast. So my brother-in-law was roped in to help get the wheels on. An electrician was found to fix the headlight. An MOT was booked, undertaken and passed. A service was carried out. The wheels received a quick coat of paint. A passenger/co-driver was organised.

Finally, on 31 May, PS1 and Montego left the Lincolnshire Road Transport Museum for Worthing. 677 was duly installed for the night in her old home, the former Southdown (now Stagecoach) Worthing garage, and Joyce and I headed off in the Montego to our former home (no, that's not a mistake) in Horsham.

Next day 677 was on display with veteran ex-Southdown Leyland Titan TD1 0813, Leyland Tiger coach 1179, DUF 179, and Leyland Leopard 465, PUF 165H, in the garage, while the vintage bus service was in operation from the seafront.

Also in the garage were several sales stands with goodies for bus enthusiasts, and from the Southdown Enthusiasts' Club (SEC) stand I added to my collection of photographs of 677's batch, and the pre-war Tiger saloons. I took the opportunity of a quick ride round the block in 0813, had a good look at 1179, and also took 677 out for a run along the sea front in the afternoon.

Worthing to London Express Service.

Photograph Mark Jefford

When exhibiting 677, despite the occasional oafish remark about fancy dress, I like to turn out in authentic Southdown white coat and white-topped cap. Chris Pearce, supervising the bus service with his usual enthusiasm, was similarly attired. Along came a well known journalist, and the next thing y'know, there appeared snide remarks about milkmen in *Bus and Coach Preservation* magazine. "Two pints of gold top and a strawberry yoghurt, please. No, that's an authentic Southdown uniform Chris Pearce is wearing!" Milkmen, of course, have nothing whatsoever to do with it – though between 1915 and 1924 at least one Southdown bus was equipped to transport milk in churns.

White coats in Worthing garage.

Photograph Mark Jefford

At the end of the day's running 677 accompanied several of the buses that had been on service back to their base, where there was an opportunity to see other preserved vehicles.

On the return journey, with Chris Pearce, other Southdown preservationists and the journalist aforesaid aboard, we were ably driven by a former driver who had been itching to get behind the wheel of a PS1 again. By the time we got back to Worthing it was dark, which for me brought back happy memories of riding in Southdown Tigers home from school or office in the 1940s and 50s.

677, of course, has the predominately brown interior favoured by Southdown at that time – brown Holdsworth moquette and leather for the seats, brownish rep for the side panels, brown lino on the floor, brown paint for the seat frames and wheel arches, brown Vynide round the windows, with cream Vynide ceiling, chrome grab rails, chrome ventilators.

In the dark with the interior lights shining from behind their jelly mould lenses, bulkhead blinds down, that healthy sounding E181 7.4 litre engine lustily clacking away on the other side of the bulkhead, the double de-clutching gear changes, the melody of the Leyland gearbox sounds, it all has that lulling, lullaby effect that soon has voices fading, receding into the background .... surely this must be 1952, not 2002 .... I'm just a lad of sixteen .... . All too soon the music ceases, the bus stops, the voices head for the exit, and we're all back at Worthing Pier in the 21st Century again. A good ride, a very good ride. And Rod gets out of the cab with a grin reaching right round his head – he too had had a good drive, a good drive indeed; he had not forgotten how to drive PS1s. We had all enjoyed it.

677 was duly tucked away again, and we headed back to Horsham. The next afternoon I got to see ex-Southdown wartime Guy Arab double decker 451, GUF 191, brought back from Denmark for restoration. She was one of the Guys that were converted to open-top to replace the TD1s like 0813, that were taken out of service in 1950. 451 was now even more obviously an open topper – much of the floor to the upper deck was missing!

What's under there?

Photograph Mick Searle

Homeward bound again we sailed up the A24 to the Horsham by-pass, where a small group was waiting for a short ride in 677. We took a circular route through Warnham before continuing.

As it was the day for the Jubilee celebrations we thought there might be road closures in London so took the M25 via Heathrow. We had never seen the M25 so empty, and 677 reached South Mimms Services so far ahead of Joyce in the Montego that I raised her on the mobile to see if she was in trouble. 677 was having flasher trouble, blowing fuse wires, which we were replacing at every stop.

In July Joyce and I took 677 to the Tribute to Eastern Coach Works event at the East Anglia Transport Museum, Carlton Colville. We were made extremely welcome by everyone and were invited to join in many extras, including a refuelling run in RTL 1050, a shopping expedition for fish and chips and later an evening trip to Southwold in Bristol VR, OCK 985K – a real flyer.

The next morning saw Joyce and me driving a London trolleybus, EXV 201, a rather awesome experience at first, because the brake and power pedals are the opposite way round to the brake and accelerator in a motor vehicle. We needed careful coaching.

Preparations for a driving lesson included washing the trolleybus.

Photograph Joyce Jefford

677 and ex-Brighton trolleybus.

Photograph Joyce Jefford

We were also invited to the pre-show briefing meeting for Event officials. 677 went on display for the afternoon, afterwards going in convoy with other visiting and resident vehicles to the site of the ECW factory – now a B&Q store – and Gunton Cliff.

ECW bodies as far as the eye can see on Gunton Cliff, July 2002.

Photograph Joyce Jefford

The following day we took 677 for an early morning photo-call at the site of many an ECW archive photograph by Oulton Broad, before going on display again.

The author with an ex-ECW body builder and ex-Southdown driver, July 2002.

Photograph Joyce Jefford

We were able to talk to a former Southdown driver who had worked in Eastbourne and someone who had worked with ECW from 1944 to 1984 and thought he might have helped to build 677.

In the evening there was a ride in the last Leyland Olympian to leave the Workington factory, followed by a return trip in Bristol Lodekka, 557 BNG, before going out for a meal with Museum stalwarts.

Next day a group joined us in 677 to visit the reserve collection, largely trolleybuses, housed at some distance from the Museum.

Lorries, lorries, everywhere.

Photograph Joyce Jefford

An interesting sight also was a collection of huge Russian military lorries that some enterprising dealer had bought up. With petrol engines doubtless giving an mpg in single figures, they were hardly selling like the proverbial hot cakes. The morning was rounded off by a drive in Carlton Colville's 1947 ex-Lowestoft AEC Regent II, with crash box.

We were much impressed by Carlton Colville, the range of exhibits, and the enthusiasm and friendliness of the people running it. There cannot be too many transport museums where trams, trolleybuses, buses, a narrow gauge railway, and a 1930s London taxi can all be enjoyed running in service. There are other cars on display, steamrollers and road making equipment, an extensive collection of tramway material, a café and shop. It was good to see so many younger people driving the various vehicles so skilfully, while the existence of a uniform blazer enhanced the impression of competence and professionalism. Certainly well worth a visit.

The event is held at five yearly intervals in remembrance of the closure of the Coach Works in 1987, and we returned with 677 to the 2007 event, which was also attended by Steve Milner's ex-Lincolnshire Road Car Bristol K6A, DBE 187.

2005 was a busy year for 677. The Southdown Historic Vehicle Group was providing the support vehicles at the finish of the HCVS London – Brighton run on 1 May, and 677 was invited to be the programme control base for the day. We duly made our way to Sussex, taking car and caravan as well as the bus. 677 stayed in the Stagecoach garage at Worthing – her home from 1947 to 1955. Car and caravan had a space on a small site at Patching.

On the big day, 677 was duly taken along to Brighton bright and early, handed over to the programme sellers, and our duties were done. So we were able to take a good look at the entries. There was a fine and varied display, representing as always countless hours of work by a great many people. For me the highlight of the day was a ride in the London Transport single deck LT 1076, newly restored by Bob Bird and his team at the London Transport Museum.

Madeira Drive, May 2005 – programme sellers' bus.

Photograph Joyce Jefford

We received an invitation to *Magnificent Motors* at Eastbourne on the next day, so duly trundled along the A27 from Worthing – no gear lever problems this time. A good display of buses old and new, and a friendly atmosphere. We were invited to take 677 to the 30th Hellingly rally later in the year.

On display at Eastbourne, May 2005.

Photograph Joyce Jefford

We returned to Worthing along the A259 coast road, including the climb to Beachy Head which the old girl took womanfully in her stride in second gear – slow but unbaulkingly. We discovered later that we had rather got in the way of the Brighton and Hove service bus, whose driver suggested I could have stopped to let him by! No way – a stop on that gradient would have undoubtedly meant bottom gear all the way up to the top, holding up even more people.

Stop at Exceat – note the green K6 telephone box.
Photograph Joyce Jefford

CHAPTER THIRTEEN – WORTHING CENTENARY

Another event on our calendar was the centenary in 2004 of the introduction of motor bus services in Worthing. A small convoy of 677, Montego and caravan set off for Sussex with three LVVS members aboard the bus, two of whom were avidly vying for opportunities to take over the driving. We decided that with this particular entourage it was worth paying Mr Livingstone's congestion charge to avoid the longer journey round the M25. It fell to my lot, solo, to take the car and caravan on that section, so if anyone on that day saw a white Montego and caravan happily sailing down by Swiss Cottage, St Johns Wood, Park Lane, Grosvenor Gardens, Vauxhall Bridge Road, Clapham Common, etc it was probably me.

24 July was the great day for which we had come – the celebration of the centenary of the introduction of motor bus services in Worthing. For 100 years Southdown Motor Services Ltd, its predecessors and successors had been serving the local populace and visitors to the town. Ten generations – or more – of buses had paraded the streets of Worthing in those years: Milnes-Daimler, Straker-Squire, Tilling Stevens, Leyland, Dennis, Guy and others. Such was to be the importance of this event, that a good two years beforehand I had received a phone call from Chris Pearce booking 677 to make sure I had plenty of time to get her ready. "The centenary of motor bus services in Worthing, a most important occasion," he had said, "and I want your PS1 there."

This time 677 was lodging at Amberley, so she accompanied the Amberley contingent to Worthing and parked up on the sea front at the Dome with the Tramocar Shelvoke and Drewry replica, the Dennis "chaser" and TD1, 873, to await events. Two years on from that insistent invitation of Chris Pearce's, here we were.

View of Worthing from the cab, 24 July 2004.
Photograph Joyce Jefford

We waited around, various people came up to look, to chat, to take pictures or whatever. After a while I wandered into the Stagecoach garage forecourt, where the 1914 Tilling Stevens, Leyland TD5, GCD 48, and several current Stagecoach vehicles were standing around.

I returned to 677 to find on board, giving a live radio interview, a former Southdown driver accompanied by his daughter. "This is Percy Randall, who used to drive your vehicle when she was a coach in Worthing" says Chris Pearce. "I thought you'd like him on board." Fine by us. Percy Randall turned out to be in his 90s; we had a pleasant chat and I presented him with a copy of our 677 leaflet.

In his hand was an invitation to something that was obviously a part of the day's proceedings. In due course I wandered back into the garage yard, and there were signs of events about to happen. The Tilling Stevens was about to go somewhere, with Bill Thorneycroft at the wheel and a number of people on board, several of whom I knew and had a word with. It was obvious a small ceremony was about to take place, with several Stagecoach managers, Percy Randall and a couple of other Southdown veterans, Philip Lamb of *Bus and Coach Preservation* and others. Then came a cake cutting ceremony with Chris Heaps, the Traffic Commissioner, wielding the knife. The buses in the yard moved off.

Back on the sea front the Tramocar SD, Dennis and 873 were also getting ready to move off following the Tilling Stevens to the Thomas A Becket. So we decided to take 677 too. While I was letting out the Dennis, 873 drove out from behind and we were left following the SD and the Dennis, which because of the slow speed of the SD took a shorter route, omitting the Thomas A Becket.

In due course all the vehicles returned to the Stagecoach garage and/or sea front according to status, and everybody disappeared to enjoy a buffet lunch for invited guests.

After lunch there was a run along the coast to Brighton, and we were told we could join in if we liked. This we did having collected three Southern Counties Historic Vehicle Preservation Trust members as passengers. Somehow 677 got ahead of the pack, and we duly reached Brighton to park up on the Old Steine for a few minutes, where we saw some of the rest of the buses heading into Pool Valley. By the time we got there they were all gone, but it did give me quite a thrill to be driving my own bus down that narrow alley through which I had been driven so many times by Southdown drivers in the TD/PD/Royal Tiger days. If only I had dreamed in the 1950s that one day I'd be doing it myself, I'm sure I would have bought a bus of my own years before I did. Back to Worthing (with a whole family of friends of ours waving enthusiastically from their front garden as we passed) – and it was not too long before 677 was heading back to Amberley.

Next day we were able in the afternoon to take 677 along to the annual Worthing Running Day, which we had never previously attended. No sooner were we on site than several people came up to greet us and driver Rod was clamouring to drive a PS1 again. He handles 677 better than anyone else I've ever allowed behind the wheel. He took her on a couple of scheduled runs round the town.

I went off to have a ride on Guy 547, PUF 647, an old friend on the 89 in my Plummers Plain days, and when I returned my own bus had completely vanished, together with my wife. Bus, wife, driver and passengers all turned up in due process of time when it transpired that 677 had been co-opted in my absence for a mystery tour. A laconic "Your flashers have gone" from Rod. He seems to put a jinx on 677's flashers. They failed when he was driving her back in 2002!

The following weekend Mark joined us. This year the SEC Mystery Tour was to be a mystery tour with a difference, the vehicles being the mystery and the venue known. The date was 30 July, and 677 stayed at Amberley for the rest of the week. In the event this proved fortunate, as Dave Bran of the Bus Group very kindly fixed up 677's indicators for us. We were glad of the chance to take a good look around Amberley anyway, as long ago when the Chalk Pits were first opened as a museum before we went into semi-voluntary exile to Sheffield in 1980, Joyce and I had given a day or two's help cleaning up the old Pepper and Company offices. Years before that again my father had been a customer for Pepper and Company's lime to spread on his fields. Everybody at Amberley was very helpful and friendly. And it was particularly enjoyable to be able to use the vintage buses as a bus service to get from one place to another around the site – very seldom does our family use buses for their proper purpose.

To get back to the SEC, on the due date Alan James came to Amberley in the afternoon to ride 677 back to Brighton Station where she was joined by 786, Eric Stobart's beautifully restored PD2 with Chris Pearce at the wheel, and of course a crowd of enthusiastic passengers.

677 awaiting SEC passengers at Brighton, 30 July 2004.
Photograph Joyce Jefford

We set off at the appointed time, and a stop was taken at Washington to enable passengers to change vehicles before reaching Amberley where we found Bob Gray's Beadle rebuild 649, MUF 488, had already arrived with a party from Hampshire.

Passenger change-over time on SEC tour, 30 July 2004.
Photograph Joyce Jefford

We had a light meal in the new Limeburner's Restaurant (opened specially for us that evening) before spending a very pleasant evening riding the Amberley buses round the site. As 677 was staying at Amberley, Alan had arranged return transport to Brighton.

Parked at Amberley, SEC Tour, 30 July 2004.
Photograph Joyce Jefford

For quite some time I had been wanting to take 677 over the old Service 80 and 78 routes from Steyning to Horsham and Horsham to Handcross, on which she had worked in the later 1950s. This dream was fulfilled on 31 July, running to the official Southdown Summer 1957 timetable with several SEC members on board whom we had told about the trip the night before. Leaving Steyning at 10.30 we soon found ourselves getting ahead of schedule, and took a photostop at Maplehurst at the time we should have been at West Grinstead Station.

Maplehurst, 31 July 2004.

Photograph Joyce Jefford

In on the 80, out on the 78. Horsham Station, 31 July 2004.

Photographs Joyce Jefford

We left Horsham Station on the 12.10 Service 78 timing to Handcross, giving me a very satisfying opportunity to stop at my old bus stop at Plummers Plain where Harry and Bob had dropped me so many times from 115, BUF 215; 528, PUF 628; 677 and other cars in the 1950s. At Handcross we pulled up, as the 78 used to do, in the yard of the Red Lion where we lunched well. Quite by chance I met a man in the street who was able to give me a lead to information about the two drivers and conductors who had crewed the 78 in the 1950-60s. This and an unscheduled visit to the former Southdown dormy shed in the village, then still standing and sound, put us half an hour behind schedule for our return to Steyning.

Outside Handcross dormy shed, 31 July 2004.

Photograph Joyce Jefford

A very real nostalgia trip for me having lived at both West Grinstead and Plummers Plain in the period 1941 to 1967. A spin off from this run was the inclusion of the picture of 677 on the photostop at Maplehurst in the revised version (2006) of David Kaye's book *Old Buses* and subsequently in the 2007 Shire Publications calendar.

CHAPTER FOURTEEN – TO START OR NOT TO START?

In August 2005 we were off again with bus, car and caravan on an 887-mile round trip from Lincolnshire to Cornwall and Sussex. This was the direct result of a small girl being taken by her daddy to a traction engine rally in 1955 – the first to be held at St Agnes, where Joyce was born. Now the 50th was coming up. If there are any mathematicians out there thinking it must be the 51st, please note 50th is right because the rally was not held in the foot-and-mouth disease year, 2001! Anyway, Joyce wanted to go, so we confirmed that 677 would be welcome.

Meanwhile it was time for a bit of work on the bus, including cleaning down of rear brake drums, renewal of brake linings and rear hub seals followed by an MOT.

We found these markings.

Photograph Mark Jefford

In due course we set off with a couple of overnight stops at other collections on the way. St Agnes is mainly a steam and tractor event, with lorries and cars but rarely buses, and 677 was the only bus on display, creating quite a bit of interest.

We took the opportunity of course to have a good look around the show, one of the biggest steam events in the country. But at times when we were present in 677 we had a very nearly constant flow of visitors. A spin-off was a chance to catch up with friends and relatives while in the county.

677 at St Agnes, August 2005.

Photograph Joyce Jefford

Moving on to Sussex, we came out of Cornwall in fine style, 677 pulling willingly up the long hills on Bodmin Moor and steadily on to our first overnight stop at Taunton, where another collection was visited. But next morning there came an unhealthy whirring noise when I pressed the starter button, and the engine was not turning. Flywheel sticking? A little levering round of same and the starter was in business again.

We made sure our first stop was on a downhill grade so we could roll start if necessary, on the second stop she started normally, and we reached the Stagecoach garage at Farlington without further problems. As usual 677 attracted attention from some of today's bus men.

Bob Gray came to take measurements to help in rebuilding sister vehicle HCD 449, which we then went off to see.

The next morning the flywheel had to be freed off again, and we again had to watch where we made our breaks on the road to Hellingly – to the same site attended by 677 on that first rally in 1976.

At Hellingly again, 29 years on, August 2005.
Photograph Joyce Jefford

Once there she refused to start and sat tight for the duration of the rally, but by the time we were due to leave for home help had arrived in the shape of a replacement, used, starter motor and off we confidently set. All went well as far as Birchanger Services near Stansted Airport, where Joyce and caravan got hemmed in by large lorries in the caravan area and 677's starter was dead on the button when I tried to move out of the coach park.

Well, we would just have to do another roll start. Fine except for one thing – we would have to roll her uphill. But there were only two of us, one of whom for obvious reasons had to be at the wheel. Now I know Joyce is strong, but she had no proven capability of pushing a 6¾-ton bus on the level, let alone uphill. An appeal to the nearest coach driver was successful. He had a load of tourists from the Czech Republic who pushed with gusto and cheerfully saw us on our way again.

For the rest of the run home I took only two five-minute rest breaks without stopping the engine. Soon afterwards I had the original starter motor overhauled, and Bruce Macphee volunteered to come to Lincolnshire to sharpen up the flywheel teeth all round.

677's starter motor, September 2005.

Photograph Joyce Jefford

It would be untrue to say 677 has had no further starting problems – but they have certainly not been caused by a faulty starter.

Fuel flow problems began on the way home from the LVVS November Open Day in 2008, requiring the system to be bled twice in 20 miles. Servicing the filter on the main fuel tap the following April seemed to resolve the problem, and the bus was started and run up satisfactorily four times during the next few months. At the end of October 2009 we took her out of the shed and the only way to restart her was to top up the main fuel filter.

Early in 2010 a repair kit was fitted to the fuel lift pump, and over the next few months she started from time to time without demur, passed her MOT and generally seemed fit and well until October 2011 when she again faltered and needed her main filter unit topped up to restart. In January 2012 she ran dry again, and we found the fuel lift pump was sticking. When it was freed off she ran well but failed again in March after using up the fuel in the filter unit. Fitting a new fuel lift pump then seems to have cured the problem.

CHAPTER FIFTEEN – TWENTY FIVE EXPRESS COACH BODIES FOR SOUTHDOWN

So proclaimed this ECW advert in *Bus and Coach* magazine for September 1947:

Reproduced by kind permission of the Editor of Motor Transport.

The earlier chapters have given the story of GUF 727 from delivery in 1947 to the present day. This chapter and the next tell about the batch as a whole.

It is perhaps appropriate to begin with a personal reminiscence. When the ECW batch arrived I had yet to reach my eleventh birthday, and the date on which I became hooked on buses lay even further ahead. But I well recall noticing their rear windows. The London service had a stop at the joint Southdown/Aldershot and District/London Transport office on the Carfax at Horsham. Seeing them there I thought how big and square the ECW windows looked compared with the pre-war Harringtons.

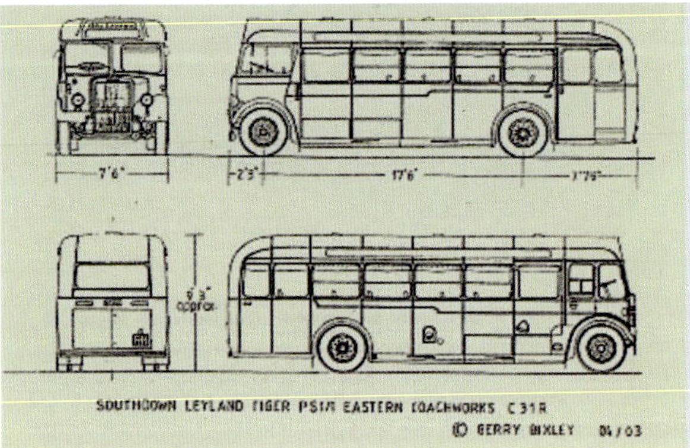

Reproduced by kind permission of Gerry Bixley.

In striking contrast the next batch of PS1s, with East Kent-style Park Royal bodies, had small kidney-shaped rear windows.

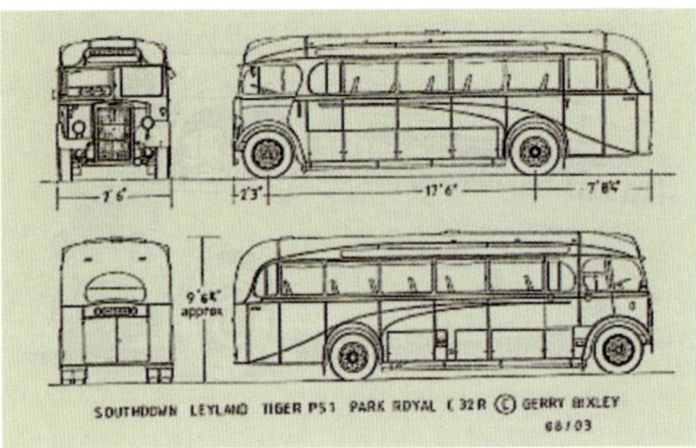

Reproduced by kind permission of Gerry Bixley.

Incidentally, one of the Park Royal-bodied coaches, HUF 303, has survived in preservation, saved by Messrs Hall and Pixton in 1972 and still within the Pixton family at the time of writing. In December 1989 1303 visited the Sheffield Bus Museum.

1303 with 677, December 1989.

Photograph Joyce Jefford

When I first began to think about restoring 677 in the 1970s I wrote to Eastern Coach Works asking if they could supply a copy of the specification. I duly received a ten -page duplicated document, foolscap size, with a heading looking something like this.

TO/JR/BW **28th October, 1946.**

J O B C A R D.

25 Express Carriage S/D Bodies on Leyland P.S.1. Chassis for Southdown Motor Services Limited.

Body Nos. 1636 - 60. Contract No. S.D. 10.

A scanned copy of the document is at Appendix B. With it came a copy of Drawing no 3862 ¾" to 1' scale, giving external front, rear and nearside elevations, interior plan and sections at bulkhead and entrance.

As part of my research for this book nearly 70 years after completion of the contract I had the pleasure of handling and reading the ECW body number register of the period, an inch and a quarter thick, purpose-designed, locally sourced, hard backed volume with pages lined and columned with the headings Body No., Customer., Chassis., Chassis No., Car No., Reg. No., Delivered., Type., Chassis Recd.. It has a line for every body produced, all the entries in manuscript in blue or red ink in several different hands, and it was a thrill to find the Southdown batch of body numbers, 1636–1660. The register revealed that the Southdown contract was only the second for the Express version, being preceded just by a small batch for Birch Bros, on PS1s HUW 780–785, body numbers 1573–1578 delivered to that operator between 16 October 1946 and 2 April 1947.

After 1948 ECW's output was restricted to companies within its parent organisation, the Tilling group, and was built usually on a Bristol chassis to four highly standardised designs: highbridge and lowbridge double decker, single deck bus and express coach. An ECW body on a Leyland chassis soon became something of a rarity, and even then it was often very much the standard product with relatively minor adaptations.

The Job Card contains many references to this: – "E.C.W. standard composite" type of construction; "standard flat floor"; "E.C.W. standard steel framed .... hot riveted" front bulkhead; "E.C.W. design" door gear; "E.C.W. OWN" opening windows; rear windows "raised 2⅝" from Tilling Standard". Indeed the whole body was based on the standard Tilling group single decker design with a few added frills, as ECW at that period did not have a design specifically for coaches. It is interesting that the Southdown cars were on the road before the Express version became generally available and in the event turned out more handsome than the

Tilling group version. This was due not least to the neater destination box and a glorious livery. The half-drop windows came a little later, and the louvres were added in 1950, which enhanced the impression that these cars were something special, with an air of solid respectability that enabled them to look at home in a fleet which had such a high reputation for quality – as some one put it "gleaming green Southdowns".

This picture shows the close resemblance between 677's coachwork and the standard bus body on the Bristol chassis – also the limited change in styling through several generations of ECW products.

Photograph Joyce Jefford

GUF 727 arrived in the fleet on 22 April 1947. We like to claim that she was Southdown's first post-war coach. But despite carrying the earliest fleet and registration numbers of the batch and the lowest chassis number and Southdown body number, she was neither the first chassis to be sent from Leyland to ECW nor the first body to be sent out by the Coach Works.

As can be seen below, the cars reached Southdown in small groups, and there seems to be little pattern to the despatch dates from either Leyland or ECW. But there are some constant factors. The ECW body number sequence follows almost exactly the dates of arrival of the chassis from Leyland. The delivery dates to Southdown follow nearly but not quite so exactly the sequence of the ECW body numbers.

REG NUMBER	FLEET NUMBER COACH	BUS	CHASSIS NUMBER	CHASSIS TO ECW	ECW BODY NUMBER	DELIVERED TO SOUTHDOWN	ARRIVED WITH SOUTHDOWN	LEFT THE FLEET
1	2	3	4	5	6	7	8	9
GUF 727	1227	677	461056	16.12.46	1654/2	21.04.47	22.04.47	17.10.60
GUF 728	1228	690	461065	20.12.46	1655/2	21.04.47	22.04.47	28.03.61
GUF 729	1229	691[1]	461071	23.12.46	1656/2	21.04.47	22.04.47	01.01.86
GUF 730	1230	692	461121	10.12.46	1652/2	02.04.47	02.04.47	13.08.61
GUF 731	1231	687	461173	20.11.46	1647/2	24.03.47	25.03.47	03.10.62
GUF 732	1232	678	461174	02.12.46	1649/2	24.03.47	25.03.47	13.06.62
GUF 733	1233	679	461216	06.01.47	1659/2	01.05.47	25.03.47	28.03.61
GUF 734	1234	680	461214	01.01.47	1658/2	01.05.47	02.05.47	28.03.61
GUF 735	1235	683	461218	17.10.46	1641/2	04.03.47	05.03.47	22.07.60
GUF 736	1236	693	461217	30.12.46	1657/2	21.04.47	22.04.47	10.08.61
GUF 737	1237	685	462037	11.12.46	1653/2	02.04.47	02.04.47	28.07.60
GUF 738	1238	682	462038	24.09.46	1636/2	04.02.47	04.02.47	18.04.61
GUF 739	1239	688	462039	06.01.47	1660/2	05.05.47	05.05.47	15.08.61
GUF 740	1240	675	462040	30.11.46	1648/2	24.03.47	25.03.47	29.07.60
GUF 741	1241	686	462041	04.12.46	1650/2	01.04.47	01.04.47	05.07.62
GUF 742	1242	694	462062	06.12.46	1651/2	01.04.47	01.04.47	18.04.61
GUF 743	1243	695	462061	02.10.46	1637/2	04.02.47	04.02.47	15.08.61
GUF 744	1244	696	462063	02.10.46	1638/2	04.02.47	04.02.47	10.08.61
GUF 745	1245	697	462064	02.10.46	1639/2	04.03.47	05.03.47	21.02.61
GUF 746	1246	681	462131	14.10.46	1640/2	12.03.47	13.03.47	18.04.61
HCD 447	1247	676	462424	06.11.46	1642/2	04.03.47	05.03.47	20.03.61
HCD 448	1248	698	462425	06.11.46	1643/2	12.03.47	13.03.47	21.02.61
HCD 449	1249	689[1]	462467	13.11.46	1644/2	12.03.47	13.03.47	??.08.74
HCD 450	1250	684	462468	15.11.46	1645/2	12.03.47	13.03.47	27.07.60
HCD 451	1251	699	462469	21.11.46	1646/2	24.03.47	25.03.47	19.07.61

Notes

1 689 and 691 were used as left luggage offices at Bognor until moved to Portslade central works for storage. 689 was sold for preservation 08.74, and 691 was sold for spares on 14.06.86.

2 Southdown body numbers were B1706 to B1730 following the original fleet numbers 1227 to 1251 in strict sequence.

The turnround time from receipt of chassis to despatch of the complete coach was a fairly constant four months. There are some interesting differences between the delivery dates shown in the ECW body number register (column 7 in the above table) and the dates received by Southdown (column 8) as given in the SEC Southdown Fleet History. Are we to suppose that the drivers stopped somewhere overnight, or is it simply a matter of differences in recording methods? Neither suggestion of course explains how body number 1659, GUF 733, reached Southdown over five weeks before it left Lowestoft!

1238 was the first chassis of the order to reach Lowestoft from Leyland (on 24 September 1946) and one of the first three completed cars (1238, 1243 and 1244) delivered to Southdown on 4 February 1947.

This is an official photograph of 1238 taken on 24 January 1947. Note the painted radiator and standard ECW sliding windows. All the batch later received chrome-plated radiator shells.

Copyright ECW Archives S J Butler collection

1238 interior from rear, 24 January 1947. Note single seat for courier ahead of the door screen.

1238 interior from front, 24 January 1947.

The bodies were billed to Southdown one by one at differing prices. Certificates of Fitness were charged at £3 a body. Later there were some additional bills for glass.

1st S.D.Body	£1367. 7. 5	14th S.D.Body	£1370.10. 5
2nd S.D.Body	£1367. 7. 5	15th S.D.Body	£1370.10. 5
3rd S.D.Body	£1363. 9. 8	16th S.D.Body	£1365.19. 5
4th S.D.Body	£1363. 9. 8	17th S.D.Body	£1365.19. 5
5th S.D.Body	£1362.19. 2	18th S.D.Body	£1365.19. 5
6th S.D.Body	£1362.19. 2	19th S.D.Body	£1362.19.11
7th S.D.Body	£1361.13. 2	20th S.D.Body	£1362.19.11
8th S.D.Body	£1361.13. 2	21st S.D.Body	£1362.19.11
9th S.D.Body	£1361.13. 2	22nd S.D.Body	£1362.19.11
10th S.D.Body	£1361.13. 2	23rd S.D.Body	£1362.19.11
11th S.D.Body	£1361.13. 2	24th S.D.Body	£1362.19.11
12th S.D.Body	£1370.10. 5	25th S.D.Body	£1362.19.11
13th S.D.Body	£1370.10. 5		

It seems that the bodies were largely hand built. In conversation with a former old hand from the Coach Works I was told that each body was built by three teams of about two workers, one team per side and one for the roof, before the two sides and the roof were brought together.

My own experience many years later would, I think, give evidence of this. I obtained some lengths of beading from HCD 447, ECW body number 1642, by then languishing in a scrapyard, to replace damaged items on 677, body number 1654. Offering up these piece for piece I found the screw holes in the timber did not match their counterparts in the strips. From my point of view this was good news, since it was easier to drill new holes than to remove screws that were resisting extraction! But I am jumping ahead of the story.

The standard ECW-style sliding top window vents were evidently disliked, and two cars were sent back to Lowestoft in an effort to find something better. In September 1947 a somewhat strange looking arrangement was fitted to 1244, (body number 1638) filling more than the top three quarters of each window with sliding panes.

The caption to this bodybuilder's photograph of 1244 at Oulton Broad reads "vehicle returned to ECW for window modifications, 5 September 1947".

Copyright ECW Archives S J Butler collection

It seems that this arrangement also failed to satisfy, as there are further archive photographs of car 1246 (body number 1640) exterior and interior showing full height sliding windows and entitled "vehicle photographed after window modifications, 4 February 1948".

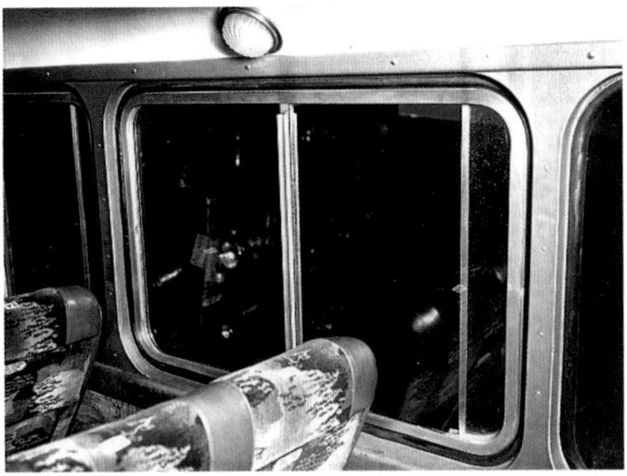

1246 – close up of modified window, 4 February 1948.

ECW Archives S J Butler collection

ECW seems to have been on a loser both times because subsequently all cars were fitted with half drop windows which, together with the glass louvres did so much to improve their appearance.

There are many publications that provide a great deal of information about Southdown – a wealth of numerical detail such as chassis and body numbers; delivery dates; rebuilds; body changes; allocations to Area; afterlife and much more. But I have yet to unearth much about maintenance and servicing or major dockings and other engineering operations. Like many other large operators Southdown ran an extensive central engineering facility at Portslade, where not only body repairs and refurbishment were carried out but also major mechanical units from engines and gearboxes downwards were stripped down and rebuilt for continued service. So successful was this that cars from the 1930s, such as the double deckers that were rebodied in great numbers in the late 1940s ran on into the 1960s and were still capable of further service.

I would love to know how many miles my PS1 clocked up during eight years of daily journeys to London from Worthing, and what was the total distance she covered on local bus services around Horsham. Certainly a lot more than the 47,270 miles currently on her odometer. It would be interesting to know how many gallons of diesel and engine oil she consumed between 1947 and 1960. And I would particularly like to have details of major dockings, as it seems evident that her present engine is not the original one. But it appears that such records have long since been destroyed.

What I have done is to comb through the SEC's news letters and successive *Southdown Fleet Lists* for the period to piece together some kind of picture of where the 1227–1251 batch served during their life with Southdown. It seems that from the beginning they were spread among all the five major Areas.

In July 1954 for example six were allocated to Brighton (A), three to Chichester/Bognor (C), three to Eastbourne (E), seven to Portsmouth (P) and six to Worthing (W plus WH for Horsham). Near the end of their working lives in February 1960 the picture was not greatly different: A 6, C 4, E 2, P 4 and W 9.

Late in 1954 Southdown began to reassign the cars to local bus routes and renumber them in a series starting at 675. The first to be so treated was 1240 which was reallocated from Worthing to Brighton on conversion. Seating was increased to 32 using seats removed from the earliest Duple -bodied coaches numbered 1312, HUF 312, onwards because they were not considered good enough for long distance work – 677's bear the number 1318 chalked on their underside. Inward facing seats were fitted over the rear wheel arches and the number of opening windows on each side reduced from four to three. The front screen was modified to bus specification and a rear screen box added with consequent repositioning of the stop light to the offside. 677 has a used ticket box by the saloon door, though there is no mention of this modification in the *Southdown Fleet History*.

Fully Converted	**Partly Converted**	**Merely Renumbered**
675 1240	683 1235	691 1229
676 1247	684 1250	692 1230
677 1227	685 1237	693 1236
678 1232	686 1241	694 1242
679 1233	687 1231	695 1243
680 1234	688 1239	696 1244
681 1246	689 1249	697 1245
682 1238	690 1228	698 1248
		699 1251

Seven more cars were similarly modified (676–682). A further eight (683–690) were less heavily modified, merely gaining a bus-type front screen, while the final nine were simply renumbered without modification.

In the renumbering no attempt was made to match the new fleet numbers with the vehicle registration numbers. A fuller description of the conversion programme is given in *Southdown Fleet History Part Fifteen* (see Bibliography).

An item that varied from vehicle to vehicle was the unladen weight as recorded in the fleetbook. Bruce Macphee noted the weights for 675–690 as follows.

Southdown fleet number	Registration number	Unladen weight tons-cwts-qtrs
675	GUF 740	6-16-2
676	HCD 447	6-15-2
677	GUF 727	6-16-3
678	GUF 732	6-16-3
679	GUF 733	6-16-2
680	GUF 734	6-16-2
681	GUF 746	6-15-3
682	GUF 738	6-16-0
683	GUF 735	6-16-0
684	HCD 445	6-16-1
685	GUF 737	6-16-0
686	GUF 741	6-16-2
687	GUF 731	6-16-3
688	GUF 739	6-16-0
689	HCD 449	6-17-0
690	GUF 728	6-16-1

I do not have information on vehicle whereabouts before July 1954, but it seems clear that thereafter eleven of the cars remained in the same Area for the rest of their years with Southdown while eight others moved Area only when they were converted to buses. I have it on good authority that 677 spent her coaching years at Worthing before working from Horsham on local bus services until sold. So she could be seen on the streets of Horsham throughout her time in the Southdown fold. Similarly 1240 would have been passing through the town on the London services and continued to visit Horsham regularly on Service 80 as 675 after conversion.

Apart from a few inter-Area loans the six remaining cars were involved in transfers, mainly in their later years. 1239 seems to have been chief wanderer, going from Worthing to Brighton on loan in April-May 1956, to Horsham in November 1956, transferring to Brighton in July 1960 and going on loan to Eastbourne in March 1961.

Fuller details of known events throughout the lives of the whole batch are given in *Southdown Fleet History*.

CHAPTER SIXTEEN – PICTURES OF THEM ALL

GUF 727

677 needs no introduction. Here she is attending my son Mark's wedding in 2012.

Copyright Mark and Gill Jefford

GUF 728

1228 goes to Town.

Copyright Alan Lambert collection

GUF 728

690 on Horsham Carfax, with what looks like Mitchell's King and Taylor-bodied PS1, LPX 729.

Photograph Surfleet Transport Photographs

GUF 729

1229 on the Bognor Service.

Photograph Roy Marshall Copyright Southdown Enthusiasts' Club

GUF 729

691 Relief. For a period a light green roof was in fashion.

Surfleet Transport Photographs Copyright Southdown Enthusiasts' Club

GUF 729

By June 1961 the seats were removed and this car went into use as a left luggage office at Bognor Regis Bus Station numbered D691.

Photographer and Copyright holder unidentified

GUF 729

On 25 April 1973 D691 was moved to Portslade Works where together with D689 she spent thirteen years in storage. There was talk at one time of turning these cars into a restoration project for apprentices to work on, but that did not materialise. She passed with the Works into the ownership of Southdown Engineering Services Ltd on 1 January 1986. ECW made a selling point of the longevity of their Long Life bodies, but even they could not be expected to withstand many years of exposure to the elements, and the two cars steadily deteriorated.

This was the condition of D691 by April 1986 when she was sold by Southdown Engineering Services Ltd to W North (PV) Ltd, Sherburn in Elmet. She was still at Portslade in May of the same year when she was purchased by Bob Gray of Fareham, who collected her direct from the Works. This photograph shows her leaving Portslade for the last time by low-loader on her final journey on 14 June 1986. She was bound for West Wellow, where she was stripped down over a period of six months to provide spares for HCD 449.

Photograph Bob Gray

GUF 730

Homebound for Littlehampton at Horsham Carfax before the original sliding vent windows were changed to half-drop. This car is said to be one of the few delivered new with chromed radiators.

Surfleet Transport Photographs Copyright Southdown Enthusiasts' Club

GUF 730

London relief – but what about Service 105?

Copyright Alan Lambert collection

GUF 730

This car was converted to carry canoes.

Photograph Surfleet Transport Photographs

GUF 731

687 on relief duty at Haywards Heath.

Photograph Gerry Mead

GUF 731

Exit Portslade on trade plates with fleet name obliterated – one guess where she is going.

Photograph Alan Lambert

GUF 732

Portsmouth relief.

Photograph Roy Marshall Copyright Southdown Enthusiasts' Club

GUF 732

Now 678 and fully converted to a bus. But is that really a Private Hire on the South Coast Express?

Surfleet Transport Photographs Copyright Southdown Enthusiasts' Club

GUF 732

Now she is a boat bus, but was replaced in this role by 698 in July 1957.

Photographer and Copyright holder unidentified

GUF 732

Poor old girl. All glamour gone.

Copyright D G Savage

GUF 733

1233 on Gosport Relief.
Photograph Roy Marshall Copyright Southdown Enthusiasts' Club

GUF 733

As bus 679.

Photograph Surfleet Transport Photographs

GUF 734

680 on Service 123 relief, it seems.

Photograph Surfleet Transport Photographs

GUF 734

Who has decided to move the registration plate?
Photograph supplied by Bristol Vintage Bus Group

GUF 734

Ex-680 on the Emerald Isle, 20 July 1965. In May 1961 she was sold to Jackson's Garage, Cavan, Eire, followed by ex-679 in September 1961.
Copyright Alan Lambert collection

GUF 735

1235. Crawley Coach Station at County Oak, long since gone, was opened in 1931 as a refreshment stop on the London Express Services.

Photograph Michael H C Baker

GUF 735

683 was the first of the second batch of conversions, which received little alteration other than a bus-type front screen.

Photograph Surfleet Transport Photographs

GUF 736

1236 heading for Worthing.

Photographer and Copyright holder unidentified

GUF 736

693 carrying canoes.

Surfleet Transport Photographs Copyright Southdown Enthusiasts' Club

GUF 737

1237 awaiting return to the South Coast.

Photograph supplied by Richard Symonds

GUF 737

Now 685 on bus duties.

Photograph Surfleet Transport Photographs

GUF 738

A pre-delivery view of 1238, 24 January 1947. Note the position of the stop light at centre rear.

Copyright ECW Archives S J Butler collection

GUF 738

1238 on the London to Brighton Express Service.

Photograph Roy Marshall Copyright Southdown Enthusiasts' Club

GUF 738

On private hire. 682 was the last of the full conversions.
Copyright Alan Lambert collection

GUF 738

"*Gleaming green Southdowns*".
Photograph Surfleet Transport Photographs

GUF 739

1239 relieving on the London run.

Copyright Alan Lambert collection

GUF 739

688 with Scarab on Horsham Carfax.

Photograph Surfleet Transport Photographs

GUF 739

Musical chairs with registration plates again, August 1961.
Copyright Alan Lambert collection

GUF 740

1240 shows destination as Worthing, but no one is there.
Copyright and Courtesy G H F Atkins

GUF 740

675 was the first of the conversions and was a regular performer on Service 80 between Horsham and Steyning, replacing the 1400s.

Surfleet Transport Photographs Copyright Southdown Enthusiasts' Club

GUF 741

1241 was an Eastbourne car.

Photograph Roy Marshall Copyright Southdown Enthusiasts' Club

GUF 741

686 was another car with light green roof, here rubbing shoulders with TD5, DUF 152.

Photograph M A Sutcliffe Copyright Southdown Enthusiasts' Club

GUF 742

1242 waiting for duty.

Photograph Surfleet Transport Photographs

GUF 742

694 on 21 relief.

Copyright Robert F Mack

GUF 743

1243 on London to Bognor Regis relief at Battersea coach park – the date on the back of this photograph is 1957.

Photograph Michael H C Baker

GUF 743

695, 25 June 1961.

Copyright Alan Lambert collection

GUF 744

1244 in original form.

Photographer and Copyright holder unidentified

GUF 744

1244 at Lowestoft again. Legend reads "Vehicle returned to ECW for window modification, 5 September 1947".

Copyright ECW Archives S J Butler collection

GUF 744

1244 has now progressed to half-drop windows and chromed radiator.

Photograph Roy Marshall Copyright Southdown Enthusiasts' Club

GUF 744

In Portsmouth now. Unlike most of the batch, 696 did move around the Areas.

Photograph Surfleet Transport Photographs

GUF 744

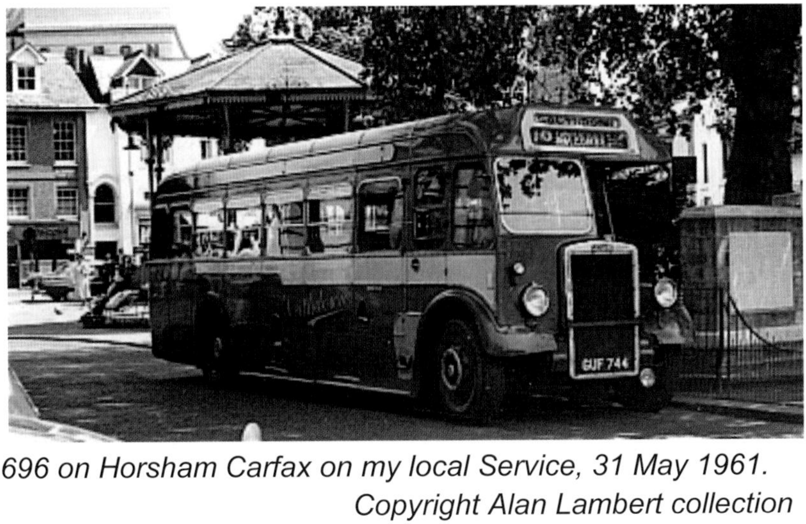

696 on Horsham Carfax on my local Service, 31 May 1961.

Copyright Alan Lambert collection

GUF 745

1245 marked for London.

Photographer and Copyright holder unidentified

GUF 745

697, now a bus – Pool Valley.

Photograph Surfleet Transport Photographs

GUF 746

1246 photographed at ECW after return for window modifications, 4 February 1948.

Copyright ECW Archives S J Butler collection

GUF 746

1246 with half-drop windows. Portsmouth to London relief, 11 June 1955.

Copyright Alan Lambert collection

GUF 746

1246 on Excursion to Tunbridge Wells.
Photographer and Copyright holder unidentified

GUF 746

681 in Pool Valley.
Surfleet Transport Photographs Copyright Southdown Enthusiasts' Club

GUF 746

Ex-681 neglected and forlorn, 1 October 1962.

Copyright Alan Lambert collection

HCD 447

676. Is this a mystery tour or just an attempt to hide? As 1247 this car was based in Portsmouth, moving to Eastbourne after becoming a bus, but she seems to be shopping at the Brighton Co-op.

Photograph Surfleet Transport Photographs

HCD 447

676 – another roving registration plate, 26 July 1959.
Copyright Alan Lambert collection

HCD 447

Ex-676, 4 June 1961 – this car had been painted light green with cream waist moulding and window surrounds in January 1959. Note also the addition of side bonnet trim.
Copyright Alan Lambert collection

HCD 447

Polly – now with County Borough of Eastbourne Welfare Department. By May 1965 the cream windows had been painted black and a hydraulic lift fitted by the emergency door to facilitate wheelchair access.

Copyright Southdown Enthusiasts' Club

HCD 448

1248 on Private Hire.

Surfleet Transport Photographs Copyright Southdown Enthusiasts' Club

HCD 448

698 still shiny bright marked for Private Hire. In 1957 she was adapted to carry boats in lieu of 678.

Photograph M J Dryhurst Copyright Southdown Enthusiasts' Club

HCD 448

Ex-698 unkempt and uncared for in her twilight days, 1 October 1962.

Copyright Alan Lambert collection

HCD 449

1249 on London to Worthing relief. Traffic volumes in those days required many relief cars.

Photographer and Copyright holder unidentified

HCD 449

On 12 October 1956, 1249 was partially converted for bus duties as 689. By June 1961 she had become a left luggage office at Bognor and renumbered D689 as shown here.

Copyright D Akrigg

Together with D691 she spent many years in storage at Portslade. Eventually in August 1974 she was sold for preservation to Clifford Jones of Wrecclesham, who also showed some interest in 677 at about that time. In September 1980 he sold her to Paul Andrews at Farnborough, and from him she passed to Bob Gray, who has no idea how many countless hours have gone into restoring her to former glory.

Bob takes up the story, saying he first viewed the bus at Farnborough in January 1986. Inside was a pile of seats which he was told had come out of Commer/Beadle 7, TCD 7. He agreed to buy the bus, collecting her on trade plates in March 1986 to take to the Provincial bus depot at Hoeford, where she is seen here in the yard alongside MUF 488 which Bob had acquired earlier.

He also says that he was lucky to receive a grant from the Transport Trust in 2010 together with a few donations from colleagues.

Photograph R E Gray

HCD 449

In May 1988 Bob moved the vehicle to his home at Downend, Fareham where she was stored in the garage he had built for MUF 488. MUF moved out to a farm temporarily while Bob started stripping down 689 but got only a small amount of work done at that time. Showing extent of rot in pillar, 5 June 1988.

Photograph R E Gray

HCD 449

Being stripped, 10 March 1991. A complete rewiring was undertaken by Bob's son while the interior panels were off.

Photograph R E Gray

HCD 449

In July 1997 she was moved to a farm, and it was not until September 2000 that she moved to Bob's present address at Funtley, where he had successfully persuaded the planning authority to allow him to build a double garage to house both his vehicles. In October 2000 restoration started in earnest. This picture shows her being reframed at Funtley, 18 October 2004 with ash bought from the local timber yard.

Photograph R E Gray

HCD 449

Being repanelled, 13 July 2005 with aluminium sheeting helpfully delivered to Bob's door by Bus Parts and Mouldings.

Photograph R E Gray

HCD 449

By June 2009 she was ready for undercoat nearing completion of exterior. By September 2011 she had received topcoat and transfers, and she is shown here on 20 November 2011 presented in her original form as coach 1249. Bob applied the undercoat. Jack Parsons top coated the exterior and put on the transfers. The coach paint is Mason's Southdown light green and Southdown dark green – same as 677's.

Photograph R E Gray

HCD 449

In June 2012 she passed her MOT test with a new set of tyres, some exhaust repairs, brake adjustments and a few other things.

Photograph R E Gray

HCD 449

At Stokes Bay, 4 August 2013.

Photograph Bruce Oliver

HCD 449

Bob had purchased moquette over the years, and by September 2012 seats had been retrimmed by Paul Toomer, who had earlier worked for Hants and Dorset. He also retrimmed the ceiling. Here we see the restored interior facing rear, 26 October 2014.

Photograph R E Gray

HCD 449

Project completed. Restored interior facing front, 26 October 2014. New lino from Nairn Bros.

Photograph R E Gray

HCD 450

1250 London to Brighton relief.

Photograph Roy Marshall Copyright Southdown Enthusiasts' Club

HCD 450

684 at Pool Valley on Service 16 relief.
Photograph M J Dryhurst Copyright Southdown Enthusiasts' Club

HCD 451

1251 on Private Hire.
Surfleet Transport Photographs Copyright Southdown Enthusiasts' Club

HCD 451

699 now a bus, but still on Express Services, it seems.
Photograph Kevin Lane Copyright Southdown Enthusiasts' Club

HCD 451

699 at Ascot, 19 July 1958.
Photograph John Boylett Copyright John Kaye

CHAPTER SEVENTEEN – ROYAL TIGER

In the Spring of 1991 Joyce and I took a holiday in Malta – to see the buses. I had read an article in one of the bus magazines about the wealth of old buses still running in everyday service in Malta, a lot of them British expatriates, and wanted to see them for myself. See we did, and were overawed. We listened, and were spellbound. We rode, and marvelled at the driving styles – clutchless gearchanges, coasting downhill, ebullient charging through narrow spaces, assertive guardianship of right of way through heavy traffic. Also a curious mix of pride of ownership and apparent lack of interest in some of the details of maintenance.

We learned that among the polyglot collection were two former Southdown cars, both Leyland Royal Tigers, one a tour bus (coach), formerly LUF 826, and the other, formerly MUF 650, a route bus (bus). We set out to find them.

The Malta bus scene was addictive, and we paid eight more visits from 1997 to the end of the old regime in July 2011.

It had traditionally been axiomatic that old buses were sent to Malta on a one-way ticket: once there they never returned. Then in about 2000 came talk of a large-scale clear out of old buses, and we learned that informal contacts at a high level had achieved the unprecedented. A former Malta bus was back in the UK. We went to see it, ascertained the point of contact and on our next visit to Malta arranged to meet the then Director of L-Awtorita Dwar it-Trasport ta' Malta (ADT) to explore the possibility of getting a Malta bus of our own.

Up to 2002 the fleet profile had not changed hugely since the massive influx of Bedford and Ford coaches, London Transport AEC Swifts, and Bristol LHs from the UK in the 1980s. Of these 187 were still much in evidence.

But in 2003 112 new vehicles entered the fleet, replacing many old favourites. Even so there were still nearly two hundred older vehicles in service, a handful of them dating back to the 1930s. The two ex-Southdown Royal Tigers were among the 44 route buses from the 1950s that were still making their contribution and were not on the disposal list. But we did make a bid for a 1937 ex-Lincolnshire Road Car Tiger, which it was then decided to retain as a museum exhibit, though it was eventually scrapped.

It was not until about 2010 that with the approaching replacement of the old buses by a new system operated by Arriva another opportunity arose. LUF 826 had by then been scrapped following an accident, leaving only MUF 650 (registered DBY 306) still in service. Heritage Malta wanted some of the old buses to be kept as heritage exhibits, and 306 was included on the list. In 2012 she was offered for sale by Heritage Malta.

In Leeds, 1 September 1956.

Photograph John Kaye

306's story begins in 1953. A Leyland Royal Tiger PSU1/16, she reached Southdown on 27 May that year and was registered MUF 650 on 1 June, one of a batch of ten with Duple Ambassador bodies for express services, excursions and private hire duties.

1650 seems to have spent most of her time with Southdown allocated to Worthing Area often going into store for the winter.

She was sold in August 1966 to a dealer, passing in the same month to George Wimpey Ltd the construction firm.

As she looked with Wimpey.

Copyright Garry Luck

She was withdrawn by Wimpey in October 1969, passing in 1970 to a dealer in Kent. The body was scrapped and the chassis exported to C Pace (Savoy Bus Co Ltd), Gzira, Malta. Arriving in September 1970 the chassis was given temporary registration number 59957. In due course (little happens quickly in Malta) the chassis gained the Aquilina body it still carries. As can be seen from the picture some Duple parts were incorporated.

As A-2908 in Malta in 1997.

Copyright David Little

At that period new buses were photographed by the Malta Police, the files later passing to ADT nowadays known as Transport Malta. The Initial Examination Report dated April 1973 gives the length as 29' 2"; width 7' 11"; height 9' 5" overall, 6' 2" interior; wheel base 15' 9"; and rear overhang 6' 7". The vehicle entered service as a 36-seat front entrance coach with Sultana Transport Enterprises at Gzira, registered 2908. In a subsequent change in the numbering system in 1980 the registration changed to A-2908.

Perhaps it should be explained that the "registration" numbers are really more in the nature of an operating licence and are passed on to the successor vehicle when an operator replaces a bus.

On 9 December 1982 the vehicle acquired the number Y-1579 and was again renumbered as Y-0879 on 11 May 1984. By October 1987 she passed to M Caruana, Qrendi and was downgraded to route bus status with 45 seats and re-registered Y-0306, which became DBY 306 in the new numbering scheme on 1 January 1996. She also received a Leyland TL11 engine at that time.

As Y-0306.

Photograph John Boylett Copyright Donald Hudson

At some time before November 2000 the windscreen was changed. By October 2002 ownership had passed to Stephen Cilia, Ghargur.

On service in Malta, 18 March 2008.

Photograph Joyce Jefford

The bus continued in use up to the afternoon of the last day of operation of the old buses, 2 July 2011, when this picture was taken in the Floriana bus station – note the damaged front corner.

Photograph Joyce Jefford

As in the 2003 clear-out of over 100 buses, there was great consternation among the enthusiast fraternity in the run-up to the 2011 changeover as to the likely fate of the remaining wonderful old buses – many of them now well past their best-before date, but still wonderful. Many indeed were the exclamations raised, but only a very few people were able or prepared to do anything about saving some of the venerable veterans from the scrapyard.

A few owners opted to retain their old buses, while Heritage Malta produced a long list of those it wanted to keep as heritage items. These were duly spared the scrapper's torch. Then in 2012 some were declared surplus to requirements and were offered for sale by tender.

Here at last was the opportunity I had been seeking for nigh on a decade. Here was my chance to bring home the one remaining former Southdown car after 40 years in exile. I bid. I won. On 22 November 2012 DBY 306 (re-registered DBU 573 on withdrawal) was mine.

She went into store for a year while arrangements for minor repair and transport to the UK were worked out and implemented – not helped by the fact that in August 2011 I had suffered a heart attack so was unable to travel to Malta to see to things in person. Fortunately a fellow purchaser was kindly willing and able to handle all this while doing the same for his own vehicle, and finally DBY 306 travelled from Malta all the way to Lincoln on a curtain-sided trailer, arriving on 16 May 2013.

DBY 306 now in Lincoln – Joyce found her name painted on the front!

Photograph Paul Jefford

So we had our bus – at last, at last, on our doorstep – a mere 20 miles away. Just put her on a low loader and bring her along? Oh no, this is a Malta bus. Nothing is simple or easy with Malta buses. We were called along because they were having difficulty getting her on the low loader. The ramp was too steep, and she was grounding. It was altogether a different time of day before she was safely loaded, carried those 20 miles and deposited in our shed. She started up well enough, but we could not move her – couldn't get her in gear. Clutch u/s, and the gear lever snapped. Nobody used the phrase this time, but now we really did have a bed of nails to cope with.

Work on the clutch has since been done, and four new tyres fitted, but it has taken a full year of battling with prevaricating gear firms to get her gearbox sorted. There is a long list of jobs still to do before the old girl can be taken on the road with confidence. They will not be finished for a while yet.

But the ambition of repatriating a former British bus from Malta has been fulfilled. We have won that battle. The cost in time and effort and money of getting her back on the road at the time of writing has yet to be ascertained.

Specially drawn by Don Vincent

When new 1650 was one of a batch of ten Leyland PSU1/16 chassis and eleven Duple bodies as below, body number 162/11 being a replacement for a previous accident-damaged body on LUF 619.

REG NUMBER	FLEET NUMBER	CHASSIS NUMBER	DUPLE BODY NUMBER	ARRIVED WITH SOUTH-DOWN	LEFT THE FLEET
MUF 650	1650	530332	162/1	27.05.53	??.08.66
MUF 651	1651	530356	162/2	29.05.53	09.12.65
MUF 652	1652	530367	162/3	29.95.53	08.01.66
MUF 653	1653	530385	162/4	28.05.53	17.12.65
MUF 654	1654	530387	162/5	03.06.53	09.12.65
MUF 655	1655	530395	162/6	05.06.53	27.01.66
MUF 656	1656	530462	162/7	03.06.53	04.03.66
MUF 657	1657	530407	162/8	05.06.53	20.05.66
MUF 658	1658	530423	162/9	05.06.53	27.01.66
MUF 659	1659	530327	162/10	05.06.53	11.12.65
LUF 619	1660	520544	162/11	05.06.53	11.12.65

This batch followed the more ornate 1645–1649, MCD 45–49, which had Duple Coronation Ambassador bodies. 1660 is included for the sake of completeness. These cars were intended for excursion and private hire duties as well as their main work on the express services. They appear to have spent many of their winters cosily tucked away in one of the company's garages.

1650 on a Private Hire. It looks like an Austin 7 in the background.
Photograph W J Haynes Copyright Southdown Enthusiasts' Club

1652 at Kingsway, Hove, August 1963.
Copyright Southdown Enthusiasts' Club

1653 going to Portsmouth.
Eric Surfleet Transport Photographs Copyright Southdown Enthusiasts' Club

1654 on her way to London.
Eric Surfleet Transport Photographs Copyright Southdown Enthusiasts' Club

1655 carrying an advertisement for Private Hire.
Copyright Southdown Enthusiasts' Club

1659 says she's going to London, and this looks like Victoria Coach Station.
Photograph John Boylett Copyright John Kaye

1660 having a wash and brush up in Bognor garage yard, August 1964.

CHAPTER EIGHTEEN – BECAUSE

Why do we do it? Chapter One contains some brief answers to this very reasonable question. It is now time to go into the matter in a bit more depth.

Why is it that mature, intelligent and otherwise sensible men and women take on the challenging task of preserving and keeping on the road machines which are designed for constant renewal and to wear out, rot, rust and crumble away?

And why of all things is it buses that we want to preserve? Surely the standard mode of transport nowadays is the private car, which is so much more comfortable and convenient than buses? Surely it cannot be logical to care so much about a bus? But you can carry a lot more people in a bus. And what about nostalgia? We do not use buses for everyday transport any more perhaps – but in our most impressionable years we did. So we give way to nostalgia.

Why again do we set out to preserve our heritage for posterity when we all know full well that the whole planet could disintegrate around our own generation at any moment? What sense does it all make?

One can cherish a pet animal and be loved in return. An inanimate machine does not have that capacity, but that is not to deny that it can in other ways repay in very good measure the time and effort lavished on it. Certainly one of the most rewarding features of owning a historic vehicle is the intense pleasure that it can bring to other people.

Take Percy's birthday. Percy Randall celebrated his 100th birthday on 5 May 2005. He was the former driver who had conducted a press communiqué in 677 at Worthing the year before. Percy had been driving coaches out of Worthing in 677's days on the London run, and her appearance for his birthday was to be a surprise for him.

And surprise it was. As 677 turned up at his front gate, complete with reporter from the Worthing local paper *The Herald,* he burst out of his front door and literally ran down the path, with his daughter Joan Smithers in hot pursuit.

After a photo session Percy came on board, and we set off for Clapham to pick up one of his mates, a mere spring chicken of 85, and returned to Percy's daughter's house for lunch. Percy held court in a big wooden armchair when not dashing up to the buffet for more food. Eventually we pulled out with 677 to drop Ernie Booker off at Clapham, leaving Percy waving at the door.

Percy and 677.

Photograph Joyce Jefford

In years gone by Percy had been in the driving seat.

Photograph Joyce Jefford

We returned to Patching to pack up the caravan, and headed for home. Once again 677 had given a great deal of pleasure to a variety of people. Another occasion that had also added to our own sense of satisfaction and achievement in keeping alive and active this sturdy old bus from the days of our own youth.

A few days after we got home we had a note from Joan Smithers saying the only person who was not exhausted the day after the birthday party was Daddy himself. 677 was equally unfazed by her trip south. The next issue of *The Herald* contained a pleasingly accurate report of the occasion, complete with a good picture of Percy posing with 677.

Joan has recently told us that he lived to almost 103 with never a sign of the usual afflictions of old age and lived in his own home until a few days before he died. Watching from his hospital window he commented that a lorry driver reversing outside was never going to make it "in that position". Percy was right – he had to have another go.

Such a sea of smiling faces.

And what grandparents could fail to be pleased by such obvious signs of enjoyment?

Copyright Mark and Gill Jefford

Then there was Mark and Gill's wedding in 2012. Mark – that's him on the right on the back seat of 677 back in Chapter Four – has appeared several times in the story already. We have owned 677 for as long as he can remember, and it came as no surprise when he and Gill asked for 677's presence at their Important Occasion.

It was a complete success. 677 was on top form and best behaviour. The bride and groom had what they wanted. The photographer was delighted with the bus as a prop for his pictures. And it was very obvious that the children were enjoying the day every bit as much as the bride and groom.

677's effect on people who are not really interested in buses can also be satisfying. One year when a group of relatives and friends came to lunch to celebrate Mark's birthday I took someone to see 677 and on the spur of the moment decided to go for a short spin. "Anyone for a ride in 677?" Within moments the only person left indoors was Joyce. Such is the fascination of that bus, that even my sister came for a ride – she who as a child was always travel-sick on the Southdown 1400s between Horsham and West Grinstead.

To enable a vehicle to be all these things to so many people it must be a runner, taxed, insured and on the road. To be a runner it needs at best, conservation, at worst expensive restoration. So to enjoy to the full the bus one rode to school or work in (or on) one has to preserve it in working order.

Some people find it even more puzzling why we should want to preserve a bus from Malta. Well, as already said in Chapter 17, for many decades the Malta buses were unique in their individuality, in their variety, in their length of service, in their constant modification and adaptation, in their range of ownership, in their presentation, driving styles, operating set-up and much else.

To rescue a former Southdown car from the scrapman after more than 40 years in exile was a challenge not to be resisted. Importing a vehicle is not something the average citizen does every day of his life, so it was satisfying to surmount a steep learning curve. A lot of work lies ahead, but will be well rewarded by hearing again that blatting exhaust note and that melodious air horn beloved of the Maltese drivers. We are very glad that MUF 650 has joined the small but increasing number of former Malta buses in the UK. I am sure she will give great pleasure to many people when she starts getting around again.

Another question I am sometimes asked is "How much does it cost to own an old bus?" I calculate that the cost of all that we have had to do to 677 and all that we have enjoyed doing with her over the years works out at £521.87 per annum, equivalent to £2 per mile travelled, or four and a half hours earnings per month – just over an hour a week. Compared to the 100 hours a week we spend sleeping that hardly seems a high price to pay for all the pleasure and satisfaction and fulfilment 677 has given to myself, my family and many others.

So the whole thing is feasible. It can be done if we want to, which brings us to another reason for wanting to – omnibuphilia. I'm not sure that there is a totally logical explanation for this phenomenon. It is best perhaps, as my wife does, to blame a love of buses on an incurable virus that had struck at a very early stage of my development – because I suspect that the seeds of a life-long interest in vehicles were sown almost before the age at which I began to have a memory. Certainly I have dim recollections as a small child of rides in the milkman's van, a Jowett, and of clambering awkwardly into a Standard Flying Something to be taken to school (I never have been athletic).

My mother was less discerning. She said it was all just a passing craze – as collecting stamps and match boxes had been. So my interest in buses would soon go the same way. Well it never has. I am in the whole business because I want to be – and Joyce wants to do it because it is something I want to do.

We are also happy to be able to contribute a little to the knowledge and enjoyment of the community as a whole, remembering that vehicles do not exist in their own right or for their own sake. They are created by people for people. It is people that build vehicles, that drive and look after them, that ride on them, carry things in them and rely on them in so many ways. So in dealing with buses inevitably, whether we realise it or not, we are connecting with our fellow humans and all their varied thoughts and deeds.

Finally as a direct result of our hobby Joyce and I have been in museum management for more than 20 years and have never seen heavier financial pressures than those that are hitting museums in 2015. Additionally, only a few bus preservationists are wealthy people. But we are all a constituent part of the national heritage scene, and there is an ever continuing need for more money and for more and more people to get involved.

If this small book has persuaded a few more of the spectators to become active preservationists, the labour of producing it will have been worthwhile.

And so to the conclusion of the whole matter: we do it because we are convinced it is worth the cost, effort and time. Anyone else want to join in?

APPENDIX A – THANKS AND ACKNOWLEDGEMENTS

Much of this book consists of firsthand accounts of things we have done with our Tigers and the places we have taken them. But I have also researched archives and read much material in pursuit of facts. I have tried hard to identify and indicate all sources and to include in the following list of acknowledgements everyone who has helped by providing information, permitting use of material and so on. If inadvertently I have omitted anyone, I would like to be informed.

I have also taken every care to acknowledge the provenance of photographs used in the book. Where I have not been able to identify the photographer, I have indicated the fact in the caption. Thanks are due to the following.

Don Akrigg – for permission to use his photographs
John Allpress, Southdown Enthusiasts' Club Chairman – for permission to use material from SEC publications
Michael HC Baker – for providing photographs of PS1s
Jonathan Bigwood – for providing details of ticket machines
Gerry Bixley – for providing his drawings of PS1s
Simon Butler – for permission to use Eastern Coach Works Archive photographs
Bill Byford and Nick Hunt, Lavenham Press – for all their help
Michael Cockett, SEC Photo Circuit – for supply of photographs
Nick Grant, Ian Allan – for forwarding a request to a photographer
Bob Gray – for photographs and information on 689 and 691
Jim Hawkins – for information about a photograph
Donald Hudson – for a photograph
John, Fiona, Lucy and Matt Jefford – for saving us visiting time

Mark Jefford – for proof reading and comments on the draft text
Mark and Gill Jefford – for use of their wedding photographs
Johnston Press – for permission to use a photograph from the *Sheffield Star*
John Kaye – for photographs from the late John Boylett collection and his own
David Lang – for forwarding a request to use a photograph from his website
Alan Lambert – for providing photographs and permission to use material from *Southdown Fleet History*
Garry Luck – for providing coloured illustrations of MUF 650
Bruce Macphee – for providing information and a drawing
The Editor of *Motor Transport* – for permission to use an ECW advertisement from *Bus and Coach*
Bruce Oliver – for provision of photographs
Joan Smithers – for permission to use photographs of her late father Percy Randall
Richard Stedall – for providing photographs and permission to use information on MUF 650 in Malta based on his research
Staff of Suffolk Record Office, Lowestoft – for help with ECW archive documents
Mike Sutcliffe – for providing Leyland PS1 line numbers
Richard Symonds – for providing photographs
Darren Vickers – for providing information about MUF 650 in Malta
Don Vincent – for drawing pictures of 677 and 1650 specially for the book

APPENDIX B – ECW JOB CARD

TO/JR/BW   28th October, 1946.

J O B   C A R D.

25 Express Carriage S/D Bodies on Leyland P.S.1. Chassis
for Southdown Motor Services Limited.

Body Nos. 1636 - 60. Contract No.S.D 10.

G E N E R A L.

1. Type of Body.

Single Deck rear entry express carriage half-cab, chariot front pillar.

2. Seating Capacity.

Seating capacity 31.

3. Chassis.

Leyland Tiger P.S.1/1 with drop rear frame.

4. Drawing Number.

Drawing No. 3662 - General Arrangement Drawing.

S T R U C T U R E.

5. Type of Construction.

E.C.W. standard composite, covered by Patent No. 557,556.
Pillars unreduced in section. Full length main longitudinal rails. Jointing compound, Black Bostik.
Protective treatment:-
Paint in accordance with memo issued 15.3.46.
Metal spraying, wheel arch cowls, step well (exterior) rear wings, spare wheel containers (exterior).

6. Floor.

Standard flat floor.
Bearers, English Oak 1⅝" wide, 4¼" deep over chassis frame.
Bearer plates 2¾" x 10 G 3% nickel steel bolted and screwed to bearers.
Bottomsides, English Oak full length.
Longitudinal framing fitted between crossbearers and joined to crossbearers by 14 G. steel brackets.
Boards ⅞" T. & G. Douglas Fir laid lengthwise.
Boards cramped in position and well screwed to bearers.
Trap doors provided for rear axle and batteries.
Trap doors fitted standard lift rings and Bristol roller locks and springs.
Radius kicking panels of 26 s.w.g. steel fitted each side of body;

7. Front Bulkhead.

E.C.W. standard steel framed hot rivetted. Framing 1" x 1" x 14 G. angle vertical angles 10 G. Cross flitch 18 s.w.g. steel, Bulkhead structure bolted up solidly to chassis dash plate at close intervals using hardwood compression blocks.

Bulkhead to sit solidly on chassis frame with slight "draw" on outrigger brackets. Balata fabric fitted between bulkhead and chassis and outrigger brackets.
Cavities in bulkhead packed with Isoflex insulating material.
Front lower panel packed Celolex insulating board.
Bulkhead holding-down bolts to be easily accessible from interior of body.

8. Rear Partition.

Arranged forward of rear entrance, partition glazed above waist.

9. Side Framing.

Pillars English Ash or approved substitute unreduced in section. Main side pillars 1⅝" on face.
Waist rails English Ash running full length.
Cant rails English Ash or approved substitute.
Built-in parcel racks supported from pillars by steel gusset plates.
Seat rail aluminium alloy supported by cast aluminium brackets bolted and screwed to pillars. Seat rail supported in middle of each bay by sub-pillar.
Standard panel adjusting arrangements.
Battery access flaps 1st and 2nd N & O/S bays. Flaps fitted B.E.T. type spring clips, and support stays.

10. Entrance.

At nearside rear 16 G. steel step well fitted with two steps. Bottom step carrying door bottom track and both steps fitted aluminium bound nosings and treadplate.

11. Entrance Door.

Outside door in armour ply.
Door gear - E.C.W. design, rubber tyred rollers in dustproof housings. Double acting lock.
Window in door glazed in stainless steel glazing section.
Hinged inspection cover over entrance.
Pull handle on interior of door.

12. Rear Framing.

Rear windows raised 2⅝" from Tilling Standard.

13. Roof.

Built up on bent ash roofsticks, sticks spliced onto ends of pillars and bolted through splice.
Carlines H.S. 1" x ½".
Longitudinals spaced to suit 50" wide leathercloth.
Housing for front destination indicator arranged in roof (see item 40).
Lift hook for gear box and cylinder head required.

14. Cab.

Built integrally with body and bolted up solidly to front dash plate and engine side shields.
Locker provided for driver, in canopy.
Tie rods fitted from arch rail to canopy at both near and offside.
Cylinder head lifting ring fitted under canopy, with extension

rod to roof framing.
Windscreen lower rail arranged to be horizontal.

15. Cab Door.

Coach type cab door hung on forward edge.
Hinges - 3 self aligning, paint finish.
Lock - E.C.W. standard cab door lock with top lever and outside handle.
Signalling window unit incorporated in window pan.
Standard buffer and dovetail equipment.

EXTERIOR PANELLING.

16. Roof Panels.

18 s.w.g. aluminium manganese alloy ¾ hard.

17. Side and Rear Panels.

18 s.w.g. aluminium manganese alloy ¾ hard.
Wheelarch panels 18 s.w.g. steel.

18. Sheathings.

Combined with glazing pans 18 s.w.g. aluminium.

19. Strap Plates.

Roof 1¼" x ⅛" bevelled edge soft aluminium.
Sides 1¼" x ⅛" bevelled edge aluminium alloy No. 24 full H.T. BA. DBB.30.

20. Mouldings.

Standard arrangements exterior mouldings for Express Carriage
Double waist moulding below rear window.
Waist 1⅛" Fluted polished alloy moulding.
Advertisement panels upper, standard aluminium drip moulding MB.269.
Cant rail moulding 1" x ¼" half round, pellet fixed.
Light rail D.R.B. 1" x ⅛" aluminium.
Cab and emergency door gutter moulding. MA.6157.

INTERIOR PANELLING.

All screws securing interior finishers (covered leathercloth) fitted cub washers: countersunk washers preferably on wood.

21. Roof Casing - Main Roof.

20 s.w.g. manganese alloy ¾ hard.
Over parcel racks, manganese alloy ¾ hard.

22. Parcel Rack Panels.

Upper, steel.
Lower, 20 s.w.g. manganese alloy ¾ hard.
Parcel rack panels screwed to framing.

23. Window Finishers.

18 s.w.g. aluminium, covered leathercloth.

24. Side Lining Panels. ⅛" plywood.

25. Front Bulkhead Lining Panels.

¼" plywood.

26. Rear Corner Lining Panels.

Aluminium.

MOUNTING.

To be carried out in accordance with all standing instructions.

27. Holding Down.

Holding down bolts ½" diameter high tensile steel. Nuts double with spring lock washers. Main bolts to pass each side of chassis frame with ⅜" yoke plates on floor and ½" yoke plates under chassis. Leather packing between yoke plates and chassis frame. Chassis frame to be tightly packed between top and bottom flanges to prevent distortion. Mounting bolts to be clipped to blocks.

28. Wings.

Front wings supplied with chassis. (Modified to suit valances) Rear wings 20 s.w.g. steel. Rear of rear wings not to be cut away. Fronts to be cleared for air flow.

29. Mudflaps.

Rubber mudflaps fitted to all wings. (N/S front supplied with chassis).

30. Lifeguards.

Valance type. Secured with special budget locks.

31. Spare Wheel.

Spare wheel supplied with chassis. Access from interior of rear locker. Standard spare wheel cover. Underside of spare wheel container not to project below lower side of drop frame.

31A. Bumpers. Standard E.C.W. across back.

FLOOR COVERING.

32. Main Floor.

Lino 4½ m/m dark brown extending up radius kicking panels. Gangway portion of floor lino in separate piece and joint covered by outer treads.

33. Tread Plate.

Aluminium bound fabric in gangway only, outer treads to cover lino joint.

EMERGENCY EXIT.

34. Saloon.

Coach type door hung on forward edge. E.C.W. standard two-piece locking gear C.P. finish.

35. Cab.

Emergency escape window in cab nearside in brass frame, incorporating sliding window - front half to slide back. Window bought-out unit, hinged along upper edge and fitted two-point locking gear at bottom edge, with inside and outside handles.

WINDOWS & GLAZING.

All glazing in Toughened Safety Glass.

36. Fixed Windows.

Fixed windows glazed with E.C W. standard glazing rubber. All fixed windows, excepting cab, front bulkhead and windscreen glass 32 oz. T.T. sheet. Cab and front bulkhead 3/16" T.T. plate.

37. Opening Windows.

E.C.W. "OWN" Combined with fixed lower window.
No. off 8.
Positions - 4 nearside - 2nd, 3rd, 4th and 5th bays.
4 offside - 2nd, 3rd, 4th and 5th bays.

38. Windscreen.

Glazing. Laminated safety glass if possible.
Type. E.C.W. in stainless steel frame. Upper half to open.
E.C.W. stainless steel quadrants and anti-rattle fasteners.
Free lower edge to glass.
Lower half in stainless steel frame secured in opening by tabs welded to frame.

DESTINATION INDICATORS.

39. Front Indicator (only).

Double exposure indicator. Top opening glazed and illuminated with Southdown name sign transparency on glass. Lower opening with roller blind and gear.

Sight Sizes.	Upper.	3'0" x 3"
	Lower.	3'5.1/16" x 5.13/16".
Blind centres.		6½".
Rollers between flanges.		3' 7".
Blinds.		Southdown supply.
Lighting.	2.24 v. 6 w. top. 3. 24 v. 6 w. bottom.	
Access.	Outside door hinged at top.	
Sighting.	Opening in back of box.	
Gear.	E.& E. fixture in box, handle in cab.	

40. Rear Indicator.

None.

41. Side Indicator.

None.

VENTILATION.

42. Roof.

3 E.C.W shell type extractor ventilators along centre of roof with C.P. undergrids.

43. Front.

1. E.C.W. hinged ventilator over near side bulkhead window.
2. Permanent ventilation through H & M vent on underside of canopy underdrawing panel and duct to bulkhead. Standard baffle board on interior modified to suit heater trunking.

44. Cab.

Scuttle type ventilator in cab offside panel, opening forward.

FINISHING.

45. Roof Casing.

Main roof leathercloth covered, Brifex L/C. S.3327/202 cream, without cross mouldings.
Over panel racks, leathercloth, Brifex N.G.R.-F.P/MC red.
Under panel racks, as main roof.

46. Lining Panels.

1. Side, Southdown Standard Rep. Holdsworths C.R.8.
2. Front, " " " " "

47. Window Finishing Pans and Pillar Mouldings.

Leathercloth covered, gold shot effect, Brifex scratch-proof, hard finish. Quality N.G.R. Grain K/FP. Colour, gold/141 red,

48. Waist Rails.

Leathercloth covered, gold shot leathercloth Brifex scratch-proof, hard finish. Quality R.W.2. Grain K/FP. Colour, gold/141 red.

49. Front Bulkhead Headboard.

Scheme as Western Welsh body Nos. 1493 - 1572.
Leathercloth covered, material as roof. Cream with gold shot effect. Leathercloth covered mouldings.
Heater trunking, leathercloth covered.
Circular communicating opening, with swing cover, to be provided in headboard, over offside bulkhead window.

50. Ventilator Baffle Board.

Leathercloth covered, cream, with gold shot effect, leathercloth covered mouldings.

51. Parcel Rack Edge.

Leathercloth, red.

52. Mouldings.

General scheme to follow standard Express Carriage.
Parcel rack edge (lower) half round ½" x 3/16" gold shot leathercloth covered.

Parcel rack edge (upper) special extruded, polished.
Light rail, wood moulding leathercloth gold shot covered.
Roof stringers, polished alloy.
Entrance partition pillar, stainless steel or polished alloy sheathing polished aluminium half round mouldings.
Headboard and baffle board, wood mouldings leathercloth gold shot covered.

53. Wiring Cappings.

Cappings over racks to be in three lengths per side, secured with minimum number of screws. Cappings finished red.

54. Handrails & Handles.

Inner edges of parcel rack acting as handrails on each side of body.
Ascending handle on entrance partition covered black Doverite C.P. sockets.
Two ascending handles fitted in cab doorway.

55. Stanchions.

Vertical stanchion in entrance, covered black Doverite, C.P. sockets. Branch extension on to waist rail.

56. Clutch Cowl.

Cast aluminium clutch cowl, secured to bulkhead by two large headed hex. head set screws, slotted for screwdriver.

57. Rear Axle Cowl.

None.

58. Guard Rails.

None.

59. Driving Mirrors.

Two driving mirrors, standard rectangular, one on screen off side pillar and one on nearside corner of front canopy.

60. Blinds.

Two blinds, Peters concertina type, both fitted in saloon over frpmt bulkhead windows.
Both blinds to have two loop-over straps to secure blinds in folded position, peep hole in offside blind.
Blinds made up in leathercloth to match general colour scheme.

61. Licence Holders.

Triple licence holders fitted to face through cab nearside window at forward end.

62. Check Straps.

Balata fabric check strap to cab door and emergency door.
Straps covered leathercloth.

63. Cigarette Stubbers.

Not required.

64. <u>Registration Number Plates.</u>

Front, oblong plate fitted to radiator at bottom.
Rear, square type plate fitted in recessed casting offside rear panel.

65. <u>Fire Extinguishers.</u>

Two Pyrene. C.P. finish.
One in each cab vertically on doorway hinge pillar. One in saloon in approved position.

66. <u>Tools.</u>

Starting handle, jack and jack handle fitted in cab in approved.

67. <u>Driver's Step.</u>

Standard step and foot guide castings.
Fluted aluminium panel below cab door.

68. <u>Parcel Racks.</u>

Built in parcel racks (as item 9).

69. <u>Used Ticket Box.</u>

Not required.

70. <u>Conductor's Ticket Box Locker.</u>

Not required.

71. <u>First Aid Locker.</u>

Accommodation by partitioning off portion of nearside rack at rear, to take Southdown standard First Aid box, as sample supplied.

72. <u>Waybill Board Rack.</u>

Not required.

73. <u>Ticket Clip Rack.</u>

Not required.

74. <u>Budget Lock Keys.</u>

1 in leather loop in cab.

<u>ELECTRICAL.</u>

75. <u>Batteries.</u>

Fitted in containers hung from chassis side members (by E.C.W.) in 1st and 2nd N. & O/S bays.

76. <u>Voltage.</u>

24.

77. Interior Lighting.

10 TAW open reflector lamps with B.M.A.C. glasses, fitted centrally over windows. 24v. 12w. bulbs.
3 roof lamps over gangway arranged as shown on G.A. Roof lamps to act as cleaner's lights on separate switch fitted on entrance partition at top inner edge. Plate engraved 'Cleaner's Switch' to be fitted alongside switch.

78. Step Lamp.

Fitted in entrance. Toughened glass. Controlled by separate switch fitted directly under cleaner's light switch on partition. Plate engraved "Step Lamp" to be fitted alongside switch.

79. Wiring.

Arrangement of switches and fuses:-

Circuit 1. Nearside interior lights switched and fused.
Circuit 2. Offside interior lights switched and fused.
Circuit 3. Cleaners lights and step lamp (fuse on switchboard and 2 switches on entrance partition).
Circuit 4. Front indicator lights switched and fused.
Circuit 5. Bell and wiper. Fuse for both on switchboard. Separate switch for wiper.

80. Switchboard.

E.C.W. manufacture, fitted on cab side of front bulkhead.

81. Signalling System.

E.C.W. standard with relay buzzer in rear partition. Buzzer and single stroke electric bell in cab, 3 pushes in body, as follows:-
Conductors bell push on rear of entrance partition, immediately over partition window and as near partition pillar as possible. Push fitted stainless steel finger plate.
Passengers pushes (two) fitted under nearside parcel rack, with stainless steel finger plates. Plate engraved "Bell Push" fitted on edge of parcel rack to indicate position of pushes.
Type of push - Dixon L.P.T.B. type.
Bell in cab enclosed in grilled box.

82. Tail Lamp.

One circular bezel fitted over recessed number plate casting.

82(a) Stop Lamp.

In glazed box under rear waist rail with Southdown standard "stop" transparency on glass.

83. Nearside Side Lamp.

As supplied by chassis maker.

84. Windscreen Wiper.

C.A.V. BWN 24/4 with separate switch mounted on cantrail immediately forward of cab door pillar.

85. Heating.

Clayton C.H.V. heater equipment (Canopy type) with interior trunking.

85A. Trafficators.

At nearside only built into chariot pillars, lower waist moulding only cut away to allow trafficators to be fitted.

86. Type of Seat.

E.C.W. Coach type seat. Provision to be made for fitting glove pockets, rug trays and baffle boards.
Centre roll of double chairs and dividing rolls on rear seat to be leather.
Seats to be fitted ¼" higner at gangway end than body side end.
All bolts securing seats to floor and to seat rail fitted Simmonds lock nuts.

87. Cushions.

Spring cases.
Cushion boards, 3 ply.

88. Trimming Material.

Moquette. Holdsworth	8140/DLY.	(Please note that the lines of shading on the moquette pattern are to run vertically & that the "bell" marking is to the bottom).
Repp. "	C.R.8.	
Hide. Connolleys.	S.M.S. D.14.	

89. Rug Box.

A rug box to be provided between the nearside rear partition and the wheelarch, with hinged door and Ivorine plate inscribed "Rug Box".

90. Driver's Seat.

Leyland Supply. Seat supplied trimmed in dark brown hide.

90A. Conductor's Seat.

An occasional seat for the use of the conductor is required, in the region of the rear entrance. Scheme to be approved.

PAINTING

91. Exterior Painting.

Colours. Southdown Standard light green, dark green and cream I.C.I. Dulux. (Drg. No. 21976) In accordance with tinted Drawing supplied by customer.

92. Transfers.

Supplied to E.C.W. as free issue by Southdown Motor Services.

APPENDIX C – MECHANICAL SPECIFICATION
LEYLAND TIGER PS1/1

Chassis Nickel steel channel section, 11" deep, 3" flanges, 7/32" thick.
Graded in depth to permit an almost consistent stress intensity.
Rear extension detachable.
Wheelbase 17' 6".
Front Track 6' 2.45".
Rear Track 5' 8.8".
Turning circle on RH and LH lock, 60'.

Front Axle H-section beam, fitted with large proportioned stub axles in phosphor-bronze bushes top and bottom.
Vacuum cylinders permanently attached to the front axle.

Rear Axle Fully floating type with offset underslung worm drive.
Differential carried on taper roller bearings.
Ratios 4.8, 5.4 or 6.5 to 1.
Oil capacity 1½ galls.

Steering Marles cam-and-double-roller steering gear.
Oil capacity 2 pints.

Wheels Front and Rear 6.00" x 20" dia, 5.375" offset, 3-piece type.

Tyres Front 9.00" x 20", LP single.
Rear 9.00" x 20", LP twin.

Brakes

Actuation by vacuum cylinders.
Front 16¾" dia x 4" wide.
Rear 16¾" dia x 6" wide.
Handbrake operates the rear brakes only.
Adjustment by RP automatic adjusters.

Engine

Leyland six-cylinder Diesel, type E.181
4⅜" bore x 5" stroke.
Cubic capacity 7.4 litres.
BHP 100 at 1,800 rpm.
Max torque 328 ft/lb at 1,150 rpm.
Oil capacity 4 galls sump – 5 galls dry engine.
Water capacity Total capacity in radiator and engine, 5 galls.
Fuel tank capacity 35 galls. Measured by gauge on tank.

Clutch

Single dry-plate, 16¼" dia x 5/16" thick, non-metallic type liners.

Gearbox

Four forward speeds and reverse.
Constant mesh 2nd, 3rd and top.
Ratios: Top 1–1
3rd 1.74–1
2nd 3.00–1
1st 4.78–1
Reverse 5.57–1.
Oil capacity 1¾ galls.

Electrical

24-volt lighting and starting.
Pin-and-socket connections at points where quick detachability desirable.
Battery four 6-volt units connected in series to supply 24 volts.

APPENDIX D – BIBLIOGRAPHY (MAIN SOURCES)

BOOKS

ABC of Southdown Buses and Coaches Ian Allan (1950)

British Bus Systems Number Six Southdown Colin Morris Transport Publishing Company

Coachwork by Eastern Coach Works Malcolm R White Coastal Publications

Companion to Road Passenger Transport History Corinne Mulley & Martin Higginson (Editors) Roads and Road Transport History Association

Eastern Coach Works of Lowestoft a Retrospect Duncan Roberts & John Senior Venture Publications

ECW Buses and Coaches Alan Witton Capital Transport

ECW 1946-1965 M G Doggett & A A Townsin Venture Publications

Glory Days Southdown Glyn Kraemer-Johnson & John Bishop Ian Allan

Leyland Bus MK 2 D Jack Transport Publishing Company

Southdown at War Colin Druce Capital Transport

Southdown Days Glyn Kraemer-Johnson & John Bishop Ian Allan

Southdown Volume 1 The History Colin Morris Venture Publications

Southdown Volume 2 The Details Colin Morris Venture Publications

The Best of British Buses Number 3 Leyland Tigers 1927-1981 Alan Townsin Transport Publishing Company

The Malta Bus Fleetbooks 2008 and 2009 Stuart Harvey Q-Nimb

The Malta Bus Handbook Tom Johnson British Bus Publishing

The Malta Buses Joseph Bonnici & Michael Cassar

The Southdown Story 1915-1965 Southdown Motor Services Ltd

SOME OTHER SOURCES OF INFORMATION

Bus and Coach magazine – early post-WWII years

Buses, Buses Illustrated, Classic Bus, Preserved Bus magazines

ECW Archive photographs Simon Butler

Leyland Trucks Ltd website – information on the history of Leyland Motors

Made in Preston website – information on the history of Leyland Motors

Buses Worldwide information from Malta's Transport Nostalgia and News magazines

SCT'61 website – photographs

Suffolk Record Office, Lowestoft – Eastern Coach Works records

The Classic Buses website – general information

The Leyland Society – Leyland Torque and Leyland Journal

The PSV Circle – Malta Fleetlists

The Southdown Enthusiasts Club – News Sheets, Journals, Miscellany, Fleet History, Fleet Lists and other publications

ABOUT THE AUTHOR

Paul Jefford was born and bred in the very heart of Southdown territory and knew the name Leyland as a make of bus years before he realised that there was a town with the same name somewhere up North. He became a close student of buses during a short holiday in Hants and Dorset territory in 1950 on noticing the very evident differences between the Bristols he found there and the Leylands that he had grown up with. His first love is for the Tigers and Titans of the 1930s, but over many years of ownership 677 has come to command equal affection. Joyce always gets inextricably involved in whatever Paul does.

Paul has had a general interest in vehicles and transport for 70 years, has been active in historic vehicle preservation for over 40 and in museum management for more than 20.

This is his second book.

Paul, Joyce and 677, Worthing 24 July 2004.

Photograph Bruce Oliver